Croner's Guide to
MANAGING FAIR
DISMISSAL

Written and compiled by
Croner's Employment Law
Ed~~itorial~~ Department

GW00598793

CRONER PUBLICATIONS LIMITED

Croner House, London Road,
Kingston upon Thames
Surrey KT2 6SR

Telephone: 081-547 3333

ISBN 1 85524 184 6

Readers should be aware that only Acts of Parliament
and Statutory Instruments have the force of law and
that only the courts can authoritatively interpret
the law.

Typeset by Concept Communications Ltd, Crayford, Kent
Printed by Whitstable Litho Ltd, Whitstable, Kent

Contents

Introduction   1

1 Legal Requirements   3

   Defining Dismissal
   Agreement to Terminate
   Frustration
   Employee Resignation
   Repudiation
   Exclusions from Unfair Dismissal Rights
   What the Law Says
   ACAS Code and Handbook
   Dismissing Union Representatives
   Appeals

2 Misconduct   17

   The Rights and Duties
   Gross Misconduct
   Company Rules and Procedures
   Some Useful Guidelines
   Right to be Heard
   Failing to Follow Correct Procedures
   Specific Examples
   Other Misconduct
   Trade Union Dismissals

3 Capability   33

   Work Performance
   Reasonable Belief
   Investigation

Irredeemable Incompetence
The Main Pitfalls
Poor Procedural Handling
Ill Health Dismissals
Health and Declining Capability
Medical Reports
Access to Medical Reports Act 1988
Access to Health Records Act 1990
Pregnancy Dismissals

4 Redundancy   53

Defining Redundancy
Reasonableness
Consultation
Alternative Work
Unfair Selection
Time Off Work
Lay Off and Short-Time Working
Redundancy Payments

5 Legal Restrictions   65

Absolute Proof
General Principles
Prevention rather than Cure
Driving Disqualification
Work Permits
Health and Safety

6 Other Substantial Reasons   71

Not a Get-Out Clause
Dismissing Temporary Replacements
Transfer of a Business
Changing Terms in the Contract
Reorganisation or Redundancy?

Customer Pressure to Dismiss
Employee Pressure to Dismiss
Personality Conflicts
Odds and Ends

7   Constructive Dismissal   85

The Contractual Test
The Main Terms of Employment
Statutory Rights
The Burden of Proof
Not Necessarily Unfair
Fair Procedure
Unfair Dismissals

8   Going to a Tribunal   97

Registering the Claim
The Completion of the Notice of
      Appearance (IT3)
Preliminary Hearings
The Conciliation Officer
Prehearing Assessments
Discovery and Witness Orders
The Role of Tribunals
The Hearing
The End of the Hearing
The Decision
Reinstatement and Re-engagement
Compensation
Trade Union Dismissals
Costs
Disputing the Decision

Further Information   115

Could You Use Additional Copies
of this Book?

Other Books
Conferences and Training

Index   118

Introduction

The law on unfair dismissal has been with us since 1972. It was introduced by a Conservative Government, modified by the Labour Government which followed and further amended by later Conservative administrations. The changes, however, have tended to be fairly marginal: the general principle at the heart of the legislation — that employees should be protected against unreasonable action by their employers — has remained unchanged and this central point is unlikely to disappear in the foreseeable future.

It is obvious, then, that no manager can afford to ignore the law. To do so would mean retaining too much "dead wood" in your department and so jeopardising your own standing in the company, or taking precipitate action against erring employees and running into even greater problems. No company is going to smile kindly on a manager who causes it to be on the losing side of an unfair dismissal application to an industrial tribunal. Nonetheless, many managers are tempted to bury their heads in the sand: to ignore unfair dismissal law and its implications, often on the grounds that they are not lawyers, or in the belief that companies cannot win anyway since the law now means that employees cannot be dismissed.

In this book we show that neither of these views is valid. The law has been fleshed out by industrial tribunal decisions and by the decisions of their appeal courts — the Employment Appeal Tribunal and the Court of Appeal — and in the succeeding chapters we show that it can be understood by even the most "unlegal" minds.

To do this, we have divided the book into eight chapters. The first sets out the words of the relevant statutes (the Employment Protection (Consolidation) Act 1978 as amended by various Employment Acts during the period from 1980 to 1992), list the categories of employees who are not protected by the law and covers the general principles of unfair dismissal law; the next five chapters cover in some detail the circumstances in which dismissal is likely to be fair, the procedures that should be followed in specific instances, and the potential pitfalls, for each of the five main reasons for dismissal accepted as "fair" by the legislation, namely conduct, capability, redundancy, legal restrictions on continued employment and (the catch-all-reason) some other substantial reason justifying dismissal; Chapter 7 looks at the implications of "constructive dismissal" — that is the situation which arises when employees leave in response to their employer's behaviour and are entitled to complain that they have been unfairly dismissed. The final chapter considers the procedure followed at a tribunal in unfair dismissal claims — how the application is made, the way in which employers can defend the claim and present their case at the tribunal, the awards which tribunals can make and the method of appealing against their decisions.

The final chapter is particularly important: while it may seem defeatist to include the section it should always be borne in mind that, no matter how good the procedure was, no matter how (apparently) fair the dismissal, the employee may still decide to make a tribunal claim and cases are often won or lost on the strength of preparation and presentation.

Finally, on a more cheerful note, it is worth remembering that, on average, only about one-third of all unfair dismissal cases heard by tribunals are won by employees. With a good basic knowledge of the law and its implications the odds should be even better for you if you have to take action leading to dismissal.

1 Legal Requirements

Defining Dismissal

The main legislative provision on unfair dismissal is to be found in section 54(1) of the Employment Protection (Consolidation) Act 1978 which states "In every employment to which this section applies every employee shall have the right not to be unfairly dismissed by his employer". In this chapter we look at three main points: the meaning of dismissal; the employees who are not covered by unfair dismissal rights; and the legal provisions as to "fairness".

The Definition of Dismissal

Under the law, an employee is treated as having been dismissed in the following circumstances:

- the employment is terminated by the employer with or without notice; or

- a fixed term contract expires and is not renewed; or

- the employee leaves, with or without giving notice, in circumstances such that he or she is entitled to go without notice by reason of the employer's conduct.

The first point is self-explanatory; when the employer terminates the employment, the employee is dismissed and so may make an unfair dismissal claim (subject to the exclusions listed below). The second point is perhaps not so clear. If a company needs an employee for a specific task which will take, say, three years to complete, he or she can be engaged on a fixed term contract which will expire automatically on its end-date, without the need for notice to be given by employer or employee. However, this expiry will, in law, constitute a dismissal and so the employee can claim unfair dismissal if the contract is not renewed (subject to the exception detailed on page 8).

The third point is even more obscure but means, in essence, that if employers act in a way that shows they no longer intend to be bound by the terms of an employment contract or are in fundamental breach of an important term of the contract, employees have the right to treat themselves as being dismissed. This subject is dealt with in more detail in Chapter 7.

There are, of course, other ways in which the contract can come to an end — primarily by agreement, frustration or resignation — and in such cases the employee would have no unfair dismissal rights since there would have been no dismissal in the technical sense.

Agreement to Terminate

The employer and employee may agree to terminate the employee's employment and in such a case there will be no dismissal and no resignation. However, such cases need to be treated with extreme caution: industrial tribunals are very wary of any attempt by employers to get round unfair dismissal law and so if an employee claimed unfair dismissal but the employer argued that the employee had agreed, the tribunal would look closely at the circumstances to assure itself that the employee really had agreed to leave voluntarily. Where the employee agreed to leave as the only alternative to dismissal, for instance, a tribunal would hold that there had been a dismissal, as the employee's agreement would have been obtained under duress.

Frustration

If a contract is frustrated it is brought to an end automatically, by operation of law, and since there has been no dismissal it follows that the employee has no unfair dismissal rights. It is, though, a technical concept and one which is of limited application.

In the past, the courts have ruled that employees' contracts can be frustrated by long term ill health or imprisonment. However, these situations will depend very much on the facts of each particular case and are not readily clear cut. For instance, it could be said that sickness is foreseeable at the outset of the contract — witness the fact that most written contracts make specific provisions regarding notification of and/or payment for sickness absence, and it may be the case that a relatively short term of imprisonment will not make future performance of the contract impossible!

In any event, frustration is a legal doctrine, stemming from common law, and is fraught with technicalities: rather than trying to argue that a contract has been frustrated, employers would be better advised to dismiss the employee after following a reasonable procedure.

Employee Resignation

This occurs where employees voluntarily end their employment either with or without notice and, unless it arises in circumstances of constructive dismissal (page 87), it will obviously not trigger an unfair dismissal claim.

Repudiation

Finally, it has been argued in the past that where an employee's behaviour is such that he or she repudiates the contract, then the contract is brought to an end automatically without there being a dismissal. Again, though, this argument is very unlikely to succeed now since it has been clearly ruled that action by an employee which amounts to repudiation of the contract still requires the employer to accept that repudiation before the employment can be regarded as at an end, and the employer's action in accepting the repudiation amounts to a dismissal in law.

To take an example: if an employee disobeyed a ruling that he or she could not take a holiday and set off for the South of France for that holiday, the employee might be repudiating the contract but the employment would not come to an end unless the employer said "Right, that's it: you have repudiated your contract, don't come back to work". The employee would, in law, have been dismissed.

Exclusions from Unfair Dismissal Rights

Even if it is established that employees have been dismissed, it does not automatically follow that they have the right to make an industrial tribunal claim for unfair dismissal. There are seven principal categories of employee who are excluded from that right, as detailed below.

Qualifying Service

Unless employees are claiming that they have been dismissed on the grounds of trade union membership or activities, or that the dismissal amounts to an act of sex or race discrimination, the right to complain to a tribunal does not apply to employees until they have at least two years' service with their employer, during which time they have been employed under a contract for at least 16 hours a week.

Employees who work for at least eight but less than 16 hours a week do not have protection against being unfairly dismissed until they have been employed for at least five years.

There are several important points to note about the way that this continuous service is calculated:

- one year is counted as 12 calendar months;
- if employees are dismissed without notice, tribunals will add one week on to their continuous service for the purpose of determining whether they have the necessary service to claim unfair dismissal;
- if a contract of employment for 16 hours or more is varied to provide for less than 16 hours but at least eight hours a week and subsequently reverts to 16 hours or more, then up to 26 further weeks of employment during the period when fewer hours were worked will count as continuous service; thereafter the weeks will not count but the service will not be broken;
- weeks when there is no contract of employment in force (i.e. when the employee no longer works for the company) will still count towards continuous service if the reason for the contract ceasing to be in force is:
  - sickness or injury, providing the employee returns to work within 26 weeks (N.B. this does not apply to employees on sick leave, only to those whose contract has come to an end);
  - pregnancy, provided the woman returns to work within 26 weeks (unless she is away on statutory maternity leave, where separate rules apply);
  - a temporary cessation of work; or
  - circumstances such that, by custom or arrangement, the person is regarded as continuing in work for all or any purposes;
- any day on which an employee was on strike does not count towards continuous service but does not break continuity;
- service with a new employer is counted as being continuous with service with a previous employer if the two employers were associated (i.e. one was controlled by the other or both were controlled by a third) at the time of the change, or the business was transferred from one to the other;
- continuous service is preserved if an employee is re-engaged or reinstated after dismissal as a result of an internal appeals procedure, the intervention of an ACAS conciliation officer (see page 101) or a tribunal claim.

There are no continuous service requirements for employees who claim that the reason for their dismissal was their sex or race or their trade union membership or activities (provided such activities were carried out at the proper time).

Age Limits

If a company operates a fixed normal retirement age — i.e. an age at which employees are expected to retire — employees lose the right to claim unfair dismissal as soon as they reach that age. If there is no normal retirement age or the retirement ages in the organisation are different for men and women (now no longer permitted) then the right to claim unfair dismissal is lost at age 65.

There is no age limit where dismissal is on grounds of union membership or activities or where it amounts to sex or race discrimination.

Fixed Term Contracts

As was said above (page 3) when a fixed term contract comes to an end and is not renewed, the employee is treated as having been dismissed. However, if the fixed term contract is for at least one year it is possible for the employee's unfair dismissal rights to be excluded. This can be done by making an agreement with the employee, in writing, before the fixed term expires, that he or she gives up his or her rights.

Fixed Term Contracts: Two Important Points to Note

- the exclusion only applies when the dismissal is due to the fixed term expiring — if the employment is terminated before that date the exclusion does not apply; and

- if the contract is renewed then a new agreement must be made, and the exclusion will only apply if the renewed contract is for at least a further year.

A contract is only for a fixed term if the end-date of the term is clearly specified from the outset.

Industrial Action

There is no right to claim unfair dismissal when employees are sacked while taking official industrial action provided that:

- all of the employees taking part in the strike on the date the dismissals took place were dismissed and

- either none of them, or all of them, were offered their jobs back within a period of three months from the date of dismissal.

Employees who are sacked whilst taking part in unofficial industrial action (ie where the action has been repudiated by the employees' trade union) have no right to claim unfair dismissal even where the employer selectively dismisses or re-engages those employed.

Employment Outside Great Britain

In cases where an employee is "ordinarily employed" outside Great Britain, the unfair dismissal rights do not apply. In cases of doubt, for instance when employees spend some time abroad and some time in Britain, tribunals have to decide where they are based: if they are based in Britain then they are protected against being unfairly dismissed even if they spend long periods working overseas.

Specific Employments

Employees in the police service and people employed as a Master or as a member of the crew of a fishing vessel who are remunerated only by a share in the profits or gross earnings of the vessel are not covered by the unfair dismissal legislation.

Dismissal Procedures Agreements

The Secretary of State for Employment may make an order excluding employees of a company from the provisions of unfair dismissal law if the company has reached a dismissal procedures agreement with an independent trade union. Such an order is only made if the Secretary of State is satisfied that:

● the procedures are available without discrimination to all employees covered;

● it is clear to which employees the agreement applies;

● the remedies provided are, on the whole, as beneficial as the remedies for unfair dismissal; and

● the procedure includes a right to arbitration or adjudication by an independent referee, tribunal or other independent body in cases where a decision cannot be reached.

What the Law Says

The general legal provisions as to the fairness or otherwise of dismissals are contained in section 57 of the Employment Protection (Consolidation) Act 1978, as amended by the Employment Act 1980. This section provides that:

● it is for the employer to show what was the main reason for dismissal and that it was one of the five "fair reasons", ie

— the capability or qualifications of the employee for performing work of the kind which he or she was employed to do, or

— the employee's conduct, or

— the employee was redundant, or

— continued employment would have meant that the employee — or the employer — would be breaking the law, or

— there was some other substantial reason of a kind such as to justify the dismissal of an employee in that position; and

● when the employer has shown that there was a fair reason for dismissal, the question as to whether or not the dismissal was fair depends on whether in the circumstances (including the size and administrative resources of the employer's undertaking) the employer acted reasonably or unreasonably in treating that reason as sufficient to justify dismissing the employee.

There are, then, two hurdles to be crossed in unfair dismissal claims: there must be a fair reason for the dismissal and the dismissal must have been justified — in other words, the employer must have followed a reasonable procedure before deciding on dismissal. It is the second aspect that causes most of the problems for employers — after all, it should not be beyond the wit of any manager to show that the reason for dismissal fell into one of the five categories listed above. It is, though, worth noting that industrial tribunals will look behind the stated reason for dismissal if the evidence suggests that the employer may have had an ulterior motive. For instance, if an employee, who has just joined a trade union and is trying to recruit other employees in a non-unionised company, is dismissed and the employer alleges that the reason for dismissal was a reorganisation, the tribunal will want to assure itself that the real reason was not the employee's trade union activities. The question of reasonableness is the main area of difficulty and it is this aspect on which we concentrate in the next five chapters.

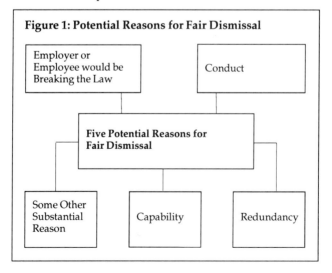

Figure 1: Potential Reasons for Fair Dismissal

Employer or Employee would be Breaking the Law

Conduct

Five Potential Reasons for Fair Dismissal

Some Other Substantial Reason

Capability

Redundancy

ACAS Code and Handbook

It can be seen, then, that the wording of the law provides little guidance as to what will be deemed to be "reasonable" in unfair dismissal cases coming before industrial tribunals. However, there are two documents available from the Advisory, Conciliation and Arbitration Service (ACAS) which help to flesh out the words of the law. The first is the Code of Practice on Disciplinary Practice and Procedures in Employment which was published in 1977. The Code does not have the force of law, in that failing to follow its recommendations will not automatically lead to a finding that a dismissal was unfair. However, given that it does represent general good practice, tribunals will look closely at any shortcomings on the part of a company and will expect to hear good reasons if it has not been followed. Indeed, failure to comply with the Code can make an otherwise fair dismissal unfair.

The second ACAS document is an advisory handbook which was published in 1987 (updated in 1990) — "Discipline at Work". Whilst the handbook does not have the same status as the Code, its guidance could influence the way in which a tribunal might judge the fairness of an employer's actions. The Code is directed specifically at cases of misconduct, whereas the handbook also covers other matters such as ill-health and poor standards of work.

Essential Features of Procedures

On disciplinary procedures, the Code stresses that they should not be viewed primarily as a means of imposing sanctions; they should also be designed to emphasise and encourage improvements in individual conduct. The Code recommends that the procedures should:

- be in writing;
- specify to whom they apply;
- provide for matters to be dealt with quickly;
- indicate the disciplinary actions which may be taken;

- specify the levels of management which have the authority to take the various forms of disciplinary action, ensuring that immediate superiors do not normally have the power to dismiss without reference to senior management;

- provide for individuals to be informed of the complaints against them and to be given an opportunity to state their case before decisions are reached;

- give individuals the right to be accompanied by a trade union representative or by a fellow employee of their choice;

- ensure that, except for gross misconduct, no employees are dismissed for a first breach of discipline;

- ensure that disciplinary action is not taken until the case has been carefully investigated;

- ensure that individuals are given an explanation for any penalty imposed; and

- provide a right of appeal and specify the procedure to be followed.

Whilst some of these points are only relevant to disciplinary issues, the following matters have general relevance and should form part of the procedure followed prior to dismissal for whatever reason in almost all cases:

- there must be full investigation before dismissal is contemplated;

- employees should be given full details of the situation and have the chance to give their views before a decision is taken;

- dismissal should not come "out of the blue". Employees should be warned of the possibility beforehand whenever possible;

- in any meeting which may lead to a dismissal, employees should have the right to be accompanied by a colleague or trade union representative; and

- there should be a right of appeal.

Warnings

In disciplinary cases, the Code states that where the facts of a particular case seem to call for normal disciplinary action (other than summary dismissal), the following procedure should normally be observed:

- in the case of minor offences the individual should be given a formal oral warning or, if the issue is more serious, there should be a written warning setting out the nature of the offence and the likely consequences of further offences. In either case the individual should be advised that the warning constitutes the first formal stage of the procedure;

- further misconduct might warrant a final written warning which should contain a statement that any recurrence would lead to suspension or dismissal or some other penalty, as the case may be; and

- the final step might be disciplinary transfer, or disciplinary suspension without pay (but only if these are allowed for by an express or implied condition of the contract of employment), or dismissal, according to the nature of the misconduct. Special consideration should be given before imposing disciplinary suspension without pay and it should not normally be for a prolonged period.

Dismissing Union Representatives

There are no special requirements in law as to the procedures that should be followed before trade union representatives are dismissed, but great care must obviously be taken in view of the potential industrial relations repercussions. The Code of Practice has this to say:

> *"Disciplinary action against a trade union official can lead to a serious dispute if it is seen as an attack on the union's functions. Although normal disciplinary standards should apply to their conduct as employees, no disciplinary action beyond oral warnings should be taken until the circumstances of the case have been discussed with a senior trade union representative or full-time official."*

Appeals

Another important point made in the Code is that an employee should have the right to appeal against a decision to dismiss. While the appeals procedure is sometimes notified to employees in their written statements of terms and conditions of employment, it does make sense to remind people of the procedure at the appropriate time.

2 Misconduct

Many managers are worried about taking any disciplinary action beyond reprimanding employees who flout company rules or behave in other unacceptable ways, because they believe that the law prevents employees being sacked on such grounds. This, though, is not so: what the law does is to prevent employers behaving capriciously in their treatment of employees. In this chapter we describe the rights and duties imposed on employers and employees by unfair dismissal law, and show how these can be translated into practical action.

The Rights and Duties

Firstly, the employee must expect, by the very nature of the contract that he or she has entered into, to be told WHAT-WHEN-WHERE-HOW to do the job (although the degree of control will, of course, depend on the seniority and complexity of the job). The employee can be told which duties have priority, when they must be done, where they must be done and finally, how the tasks should be done. If he or she does not come up to standard or is disobedient the employer can take disciplinary action, or for serious matters, dismiss the employee. The employee has no effective way of resisting: if the employer has a legitimate reason for taking such action the employee has to submit to it. No court or tribunal will force an employer to go on employing the employee nor will it normally interfere in internal disciplinary proceedings.

Secondly, the employer should realise that these rights are limited by the terms and conditions of the contract as they were agreed and by whether or not the order is a lawful and reasonable one that will not place the employee in danger when it is carried out. Consequently, the employer cannot usually tell the employee to go and do some gardening if the employee holds the job of chief engineer. The employer can ask for and obtain the employee's agreement but should not issue an order.

An employee who is a bricklayer cannot be required to repoint the top layer of bricks of a 400ft factory chimney unless he or she is specifically employed to do the job, has accepted the danger involved or has agreed to do the work. The employer must also be sure that the person is skilful and experienced enough to do it.

The order given by the employer must also be reasonable. To employ maintenance engineers on long standby hours so that they cannot rest would be an unreasonable action by the employer. Similarly, to order an employee known to have back trouble to lift a heavy weight would be unreasonable even if it was work the employee was normally required to do.

Obviously, in day to day practice employers do not go around issuing commands and expecting everyone to jump. Employees are asked to carry out work and persuasion is often used.

Gross Misconduct

As already indicated, not all misconduct is of the same severity and consequently the employer will not seek to dismiss immediately for minor breaches of company rules. This sanction will normally be reserved for what is termed "gross misconduct". Such acts can vary between different companies and where there are written rules they are often listed and specifically classified as offences for which summary dismissal is the penalty. However, some actions are universally thought of as being gross misconduct — theft, fraud, insubordination, physical violence, refusal to carry out a reasonable order, etc. These actions by the employee go to the root of the employment relationship.

The employee's action, whatever it is, must destroy the employment relationship. There may, however, be circumstances in which the relationship can still survive and continue in spite of obvious acts of gross misconduct on the employee's part. For instance, employers can and do continue to employ a person who has committed an act of theft if there is reason to believe it was an out-of-character, momentary lapse and it is pretty certain that it will not happen again. Whatever the reason, the employer may choose not to use the ultimate sanction of dismissal but retain the employee under the final written warning so that the matter is not completely forgotten.

The fact is, employers can act perfectly reasonably if they take either course of action providing all the circumstances have been properly considered. This is why an industrial tribunal does not stop and say that there is no case to answer when the employer proves there has been an act of gross misconduct. The tribunal must go on to consider how the employer arrived at the decision and whether it was fair in all the circumstances of the case. The two crucial elements in a procedure to deal with gross misconduct cases are proper investigation and allowing the employee to state his or her case. More about this later.

Company Rules and Procedures

Normally company disciplinary procedures are not very helpful to a manager trying to deal with theft or other forms of dishonesty.

"Stealing or other acts of dishonesty will result in summary dismissal without notice" is usually all that is said. The rules do not say that the employee will be dismissed if the responsible manager has a reasonable belief in the employee's guilt nor that it will not be necessary to prove that guilt beyond all reasonable doubt. Neither do the procedures state how a summary dismissal should be carried out. This poses a dilemma for managers who do not come across this kind of problem on a day to day basis.

Even when an employer has a rule which outlaws specific kinds of conduct and states that the offence will result in summary dismissal, it is unwise to jump without taking time for reflection. In such cases, tribunals are still obliged to see if the employer has acted reasonably in treating the broken rules as sufficient reason for dismissal and whether the rule was reasonable. Of course, the rules must have been brought to the attention of employees for them to have any standing at all.

For a start, does the punishment fit the crime? In one company there was a rule stating that smoking in a no-smoking area would result in dismissal. An employee wandered inadvertently into such an area with a cigarette and put it out immediately when he was told. His subsequent dismissal was unfair in the circumstances. However, in another case a petroleum tanker driver lit up a cigarette at a delivery point, in breach of the delivery procedure rules. In the circumstances this dismissal was fair because one breach could have a catastrophic effect and a further lapse could not be risked.

Another point to be considered is whether the rule is relevant to the type of job the employee was employed to do. A worker employed as a labourer in a gravel pit was dismissed for failing to wear a tie or have his hair cut. Rubbish, said the tribunal: this was an inappropriate rule to apply to the employment and consequently the dismissal was unfair.

The question of whether the rule has been consistently applied, or has been used in a particular case with no apparent justification, will also affect the fairness of a subsequent dismissal, as will the situation where a rule has fallen into disuse only to be resurrected again to justify dismissal. Where the rule has been waived with such regularity that the employees have been lulled into a false sense of security, the dismissal will be unfair.

This does not, though, mean that the employer must enforce the rules and mete out the same punishment regardless of the surrounding circumstances. The employer should look at the facts of the individual case and may be justified in taking different actions for different people. For instance, if the rule states that employees caught fighting will be summarily dismissed, it would be entirely wrong to apply the rule without further investigation and consideration of mitigating circumstances. Perhaps the employee was provoked, or has many years of unblemished service, or it was just a technical assault — not really a bad fight and it did not happen in a dangerous place near machinery or chemicals — or the protagonists were of equal status, etc. Any of these factors may call for a lesser penalty than dismissal — a final warning, demotion or suspension without pay (if the employee's contract allows). This will not prejudice future dismissals under the ruling unless the employees are led to believe that the rule will never be enforced by dismissal in future cases with parallel circumstances.

Finally, is the rule clear and unambiguous or is it drafted in such a way that the employee may be misled? For instance, if it states that an employee may be dismissed for one breach of the rules, employees could reasonably believe that breach of the rule would not lead to dismissal without prior warning. Better to spell out that dismissal will result.

Some Useful Guidelines

As previously emphasised, proper investigation is essential. It is on the facts discovered in this way that the manager will base his or her reasonable belief. So, what evidence is there to suggest that the employee is, for example, stealing? Is someone pointing the finger? Is it hearsay, i.e. another employee has reported that the person concerned had told him or her about stealing the equipment? Does circumstantial evidence point towards guilt? There may be several explanations of the events but if the only convincing one, on the balance of probabilities, is that the employee has been stealing — for instance, it is the sixth time that theft has occurred when that person has been in sole charge of the warehouse — then there will be reasonable grounds for believing in that person's guilt. This is not the sort of evidence on which a criminal court could convict but the standard of proof required by an industrial tribunal is quite different from that in criminal proceedings.

It may be tempting to bring in the police to investigate, but this does not absolve managers from the necessity of carrying out their own investigation. It is, after all, the employer who has to decide whether to dismiss the employee — the police are bringing a criminal action in the court and it is not unknown for people to be acquitted on technicalities which have little or nothing to do with the merits of the case. The employee can be suspended on pay whilst the investigation is carried out. Do not delay too long, though. In one case a company waited for a report from an in-store detective and then carried on building up a case against the employee. She was not challenged about till irregularities for some time. In her subsequent unfair dismissal claim the tribunal decided that the dismissal was unfair because the delay meant that she could not realistically recall the purchase on which the allegation rested, and therefore had no basis on which to defend herself.

Thefts can vary considerably in size and implication. A series of petty acts such as purloining items of stationery can provide a fair reason for dismissal provided warnings have been given. If managerial staff commit some small financial irregularity, their position of trust is undermined — the more senior the employee is, the more serious the offence becomes, and dismissal for petty matters can be fair. Where these acts break important procedural rules but do not involve actual theft, dismissal may still be fair. For example, a manager borrowed some money from the till, and put in an IOU for the appropriate amount, so that he could place a bet on a horse. This action was sufficient to destroy the employer's trust in the employee, and so his dismissal was not unfair.

Right to be Heard

Once the manager is sure of the facts he or she must call the employee back from suspension and place these facts before the employee at a disciplinary hearing. If the employee wishes to be accompanied, this should be allowed. Firstly, the manager will be checking the facts against what the employee says has happened. The employee should be shown any evidence against him or her and be given the opportunity to question the accuser. Secondly, the manager should investigate further if any of the employee's explanations have a ring of truth to them. Thirdly, the manager should tell the employee what interpretation is being put on the facts — even if it means saying "I think you are taking company property away from the premises without permission" or "I believe you are stealing from stock" — although, of course, such an allegation would constitute slander unless it could be justified. Fourthly, the employee should be asked to explain his or her conduct adequately. The employee should be told to think carefully about this explanation and told that dismissal will be the outcome unless there are any mitigating factors which should be taken into account.

Even if employees are caught redhanded they should be allowed to explain themselves — in effect, to petition to keep the job because of mitigating circumstances. There is, after all, a whole world of difference between the person who didn't believe he or she was actually acting dishonestly when taking the scrap or cut-off pieces, and the systematic semi-professional who is taking materials from the employer and making a business out of selling them. Ideally, the interview should be carried out by the manager who will take the decision to dismiss.

It is rarely a good idea to delay the decision until the outcome of criminal proceedings is known. Bear in mind the different functions of criminal proceedings and disciplinary employment proceedings. A criminal court must establish beyond all reasonable doubt that a criminal offence has been committed whereas an employer must establish a reasonable belief on reasonable grounds that the employee has committed a breach of the company's disciplinary code. It follows therefore than an employee could be fairly dismissed but found to be not guilty by the criminal court. Beware! If the employee is being held in custody and the trial keeps being postponed, it is tempting to make a decision anyway. In such a case, it is still important to get the employee's representations, usually via his or her solicitor, before the decision is made. It should also be made clear that the decision to dismiss has been triggered by the manning difficulties as a result of absence, and is not due to a change of mind. In all cases employees should be told of their right of appeal (see ACAS Code of Practice on page 12).

Failing to Follow Correct Procedures

There have been cases in the past where a failure to investigate or to allow the employee to state his or her case have not caused a subsequent dismissal to be unfair!

Usually this was on the basis that if the procedure had been properly followed, dismissal would still have been the outcome. However, this approach has now been ruled incorrect and the need to follow fair procedures has been restated. Essentially, an employer who fails to investigate or give an opportunity for comment by an employee, or who fails to give prior warnings where necessary can expect a finding of unfair dismissal. It is no use maintaining that the employee would still have been dismissed had proper procedures been followed and expecting to be left off the hook. It would only be where an employer had **reasonably** decided that following the procedure would be completely worthless that a tribunal may find dismissal fair. These instances will be extremely rare.

Specific Examples

Working in Competition: Employees must not misuse trade secrets or confidential information that they come across during their employment. This is a common law obligation and often a requirement that is expressly stated in the contract of employment.

Spare time work for another employer may be prohibited by a clause in the contract of employment except, for example where written permission is given. Normally, however, work for a competing employer will be grounds for dismissal if there is a substantial chance of confidential know-how and information being passed on. Similarly, if the employee sets up in business, even in a small way, to cream off work in the same geographicala rea as the employer, this will constitute grounds for dismissal.

However, where an employee is merely contemplating this action rather than actually having made a start on it, this would not in itself form grounds for dismissal.

Once again, the matter must be carefully investigated, but the burden of proof is still one of reasonable belief, and allowing employees to state their case is the other important element in handling this sort of dismissal correctly. The following checklist summarises the factors that the manager should take into account.

Checklist: Working in Competition

- has the employee tried to keep the spare time work a secret;

- is the employee truly working for a competitor or as a competitor;

- is the employee employed in a capacity where this work could harm the company;

- does the employee have access to confidential information; and

- is the employee trying to entice away other employees?

Sometimes the employee is not working in competition but has such enormous outside commitments to, say, particular hobbies or sports or the family business, etc., that work for the employer suffers. The employer has every right to take the employee to task if his or her performance drops off at work. The employee should be warned in writing, perhaps given the chance to loosen some of those commitments, and be told that dismissal will result if there is no improvement.

It is important to note that this is not a situation where summary dismissal without notice can be used unless employees refuse a reasonable order, for instance they refuse to do contractual overtime.

Disobeying Orders: If the manager has an employee who refuses to carry out an order, he or she is well advised to consider the following points in the checklist overleaf.

Providing the instruction was a reasonable one, within the terms of the employee's duties, and the employee had no satisfactory reason for refusing, the manager can insist that the instruction must be carried out or else disciplinary action will be taken. This may take the form of a final warning or even dismissal depending on the nature of the instruction and the reason for the employee's refusal.

Checklist: Disobeying Orders

- was the employee given a legitimate instruction, was it lawful, was it reasonable, would the employee be placed in a dangerous situation, was the instruction to carry out duties that are part of the employee's contract;

- was the instruction given clearly so that the employee would understand;

- did the manager listen to the employee's reasons for not carrying out the instruction: why did the employee disobey the instruction?

Overtime: If an employee is required to work overtime, but refuses point blank to do so, the manager must be sure of the contractual right to insist that overtime be worked, or that there is such an overriding necessity (as opposed to convenience) for the overtime to be worked that the reasonable employee would co-operate (e.g. completion of an order or a penalty clause on the contract that would cost the employer dear), before taking disciplinary action. Even if the employee frequently works overtime this does not automatically mean that there is a contractual right to require overtime to be worked.

The reason for the refusal must also be taken into account. If the employee is just "standing on the terms of the contract", ie "I don't have to do overtime unless I agree", "You've no right to force me", then his or her refusal may not be viewed sympathetically by a tribunal. Was the employee given enough warning of the overtime or was it an emergency? Was there some prior arrangement to take a relative to hospital, or look after the children that dictated refusal because no other arrangement could be made?

These are the sort of factors that justify a refusal — providing that it does not happen over and over again, especially where overtime is distributed on a rostered basis and collective discipline may suffer. The manager's decision to dismiss in these circumstances must be reasonable in all the circumstances taking the following factors into consideration:

- has the employee's action been condoned before;
- has the employee got long and exemplary service;
- was dismissal too harsh a punishment;
- have other employees been treated differently when they refused to work overtime?

Tribunals will make allowances for smaller companies; they recognise the impossible position that they are put into if an employee is intransigent and unco-operative. In one case an employee with 36 years' service was fairly dismissed when he consistently refused to fix wooden chairs (occasionally part of his duties) because he had a row with the boss's son who had just come into the business.

The procedure used before dismissal is also crucial. The procedure does not have to be slow: for instance, a welder refused, in no uncertain terms, to carry out work in a place where he said there was a fumes hazard. He was offered a mask which he would not accept, and after refusing again he was warned what he would be dismissed. He continued with his refusal and was dismissed. It was not unfair.

Other Misconduct

Most acts of misconduct which confront managers, however, are not so dramatic. They are faced with employees who are annoying rather than employees who behave spectacularly badly — often the employees are only testing the water to see how far they can go; what concessions they can get. In such cases dismissal is inappropriate in the early stages and would be unfair in almost every case. Employers are expected to try to bring the employee back into line (see the ACAS Code of Practice on page 12).

Once again the employer's actions are judged according to the facts of each case and it can be dangerous to adopt standard solutions without making allowances for the individual facts. However, certain principles, outlined in the next checklist will almost always apply.

Checklist: Handling Misconduct

- investigate the matter and give the employee a chance to say what happened so that differences in the story can be properly checked;the employee should be given the chance to explain why he or she acted in that way and to present any mitigating circumstances;

- the employee should be warned of the consequences of further misconduct and then given a realistic opportunity to improve;

- the employer should consider whether some other penalty is appropriate, eg demotion, transfer, suspension, etc. (provided such penalty is authorised by the contract or the employee agrees to it); and

- the employee should be informed of the right of appeal.

Detailed advice on appropriate procedures for different types of misconduct is set out in *Croner's Guide to Managing Discipline* but guidelines dealing with the most common problems are set out below.

Appropriate Procedures

Clothes and Appearance: Employers have the right to frame reasonable standards of dress for their employees to follow, eg normal business dress in white collar employment, or rules relating to safety and hygiene, covering matters such as long hair not tied back when working near machinery or casual shoes without toe pieces in a warehouse. Employers can require company uniforms to be worn by their employees, though it is debatable whether they can require payment for them if this is not an original term of the contract.

Employers should keep their rules updated in line with changing standards — for instance, the sight of a man wearing an earring is not nearly so outlandish nowadays as it once was. The manager's personal dislike of a particular style may be unreasonable. The test is whether a reasonable employer in the same employment situation would find the style unacceptable. The employee should be warned that his or her conduct — perhaps in coming to work in jeans and a teeshirt — will result in dismissal unless a more conventional office style is adopted.

Time-Keeping and Absenteeism: Poor time-keeping and absenteeism do not usually amount to gross misconduct and consequently the employee should receive warnings (providing the problem is one of conduct rather than capability) before dismissal. Indeed, the employee should be given the chance to improve over a period of time during which any response to the warning can be assessed. It is unwise to dismiss at the next offence — it will probably be the one time that the employee has a justifiable reason for being late or absent!

Warning does not mean "chivvying" or telling someone to "buck up your ideas". The employee should be interviewed with the aim of establishing why this poor standard of time-keeping or absenteeism has arisen and should be told what is an acceptable standard. The employee must then be given a period of time in which to improve. No further disciplinary action should be taken until the end of that period, although the employee's behaviour should be closely monitored by the manager throughout, and the employee should be challenged whenever he or she is late and asked for any excuses. These should, of course, be checked as soon as possible.

An employee with more than two years' service is entitled to a written statement giving reasons for dismissal. If requested this statement must be provided by the employer within 14 days. The precedent letter set out at the end of this chapter illustrates further the importance of being able to record that clear warnings and a chance to improve has been given.

Trade Union Dismissals

Special rules apply to employees who are dismissed for trade union membership or activities. Employees will be unfairly dismissed if the reason is their trade union membership or non-membership or trade union activities. The burden of proving that dismissal was for such a reason lies with the employee if he or she has less than two years' service, but for practical purposes the employer should be able to show that there was some other reason for dismissal, unconnected with union membership or activities. The burden of proof lies with the employer if the employee has got more than two years' service.

Very often the problem is caused by an employee trying to recruit other employees into union membership at the wrong time. Recruitment is a union activity but the law requires it to be carried out at "an appropriate time", ie outside working hours or within working hours in accordance with agreed arrangements or with the consent of the employer. For instance, talking to other employees about the advantages of union membership during tea breaks or whilst still operating machinery in accordance with normal custom has been held by tribunals to be union activity at an appropriate time.

If the employee oversteps the line and is caught in a huddle with other employees, or interrupting their work during normal working hours, he or she should be warned first of the infringement and be told to seek the advice of the union. The normal disciplinary procedure would then apply. It is a good idea to play safe because dismissing employees on these grounds is very costly indeed, much more so than in normal unfair dismissal cases (see Special Award, page 110), not to mention the damage that may be caused to industrial relations.

**Example: Letter giving Written Reasons for Dismissal
Misconduct — Timekeeping**

Dear Mr Brown

Further to your request for written reasons for dismissal
we confirm that the reason was your inadequate
time-keeping. Over the last six months you received
numerous verbal warnings and two written warnings
(copies enclosed) concerning your failure to attend work
promptly at 9.00 am each day.

There was no improvement and you agreed that there
was no adequate reason for your poor attendance —
except that you "couldn't get up in the morning".

You are aware that good time-keeping is expected of all
staff and your record was considerably worse than that
of any other person in the company.

In these circumstances you were given one month's
notice by your manager to terminate your employment
for the reason stated above.

3 Capability

Capability is defined as skill, aptitude, health or any other physical or mental quality. It follows, then, that it can be potentially ''fair'' to dismiss people if they can no longer cope, whatever the reason: failing health, mental illness, old-age or perhaps because standards have been raised. The fairness of the dismissal will depend on the type of procedure followed before dismissal. See Figure 2 at the end of this chapter.

Work Performance

There is an enormous range of work performance problems, of which the commonest examples are:

- employees who couldn't care less and who deliberately work as slowly as possible. Here, investigation of the situation will point to this being a conduct matter rather than any innate incapability to do the job in an acceptable manner. The disciplinary warnings should confirm that emphasis. The employer/employee relationship requires the employee to work to full capacity and not to limit his or her effort (it is implied into every contract of employment), hence the legitimacy of such a warning;

- employees who are difficult and refuse to believe that their performance is unacceptable or that their personalities are completely unsuited to the job they are required to do or to a particular working environment. Employees can be required to co-operate with their employer, which implies obeying reasonable instructions and generally helping to further the aims of the organisation; when their attitude conflicts with this. The employer is justified in giving the employee a warning. In many cases it would have to be accepted that the employee cannot change his or her personality and unless a more suitable job can be found dismissal will be the ultimate result. For instance, one employee was considered "competent and experienced", had a detailed knowledge of building law, and was loyal, conscientious and meticulous, but he did not get on well with customers because he was unco-operative and unbending. It was not in his nature to be flexible and he was fairly dismissed for incapability because he did not have the necessary aptitude and mental qualities for the job of contracts manager;

- employees who are unable to reach raised standards now required by the employer. It is important that employees should know from the outset that the ball-game has changed, and they should be given a clear idea of the standard that is expected and some retraining of appropriate. The warning procedure can then begin if these standards are not achieved. Make sure that the standards required are not unreasonable and, on the whole, are attainable by the majority of other employees doing the job;

- employees with some physical disability that prevents them from doing the job adequately, eg colour blindness in an apprentice electrician; and

- employees who are irredeemably incompetent.

Reasonable Belief

The burden of proof at a tribunal hearing is on the employer to show that there was good reason to believe that the employee was incapable. The starting point, then is: who says the employee is no good? Very often it is the manager's opinion, but what evidence is there to support it? How far must they go to establish that the employee is not very good at the job so that a tribunal will be satisfied? In order to satisfy the "reasonable belief" test the employer must show that there are grounds for the reasonable belief: he or she must have taken reasonable steps to verify those beliefs or, in other words, conducted a proper investigation. It is not necessary for the employer to prove in fact (beyond all reasonable doubt) that the employee is incapable or incompetent. Employers are the best judges of a person's capability in their particular specialised fields, providing that their judgement has not been swayed by, for instance, personal likes and dislikes.

Investigation

It is sometimes easy to attach performance measures and to monitor the situation: bench workers whose work is booked in and out, whose inaccurate work is noted and records are kept, can be easily assessed. So too with sales representatives, piece workers, packers, etc. However, after establishing that the performance of one employee is worse than that of other employees, the investigation does not end. Are these performance standards realistic? Are there any external factors outside the employee's control which are affecting his or her performance, eg a new competitor in the field, poor machinery maintenance resulting in downtime or poor organisation of materials, etc? What does the employee give as the reasons for the poor performance? Check them and if there is no real weight to the excuses explain to the employee why they are discounted. Careful investigation means analysis of the employee's strengths and weaknesses, to see where he or she is going wrong.

For instance, what does it mean to say that someone is a "poor sales representative"? Is the employee not putting enough effort into making an acceptable number of calls each week; is there failure to follow up orders; is the employee plodding along with existing customers and failing to develop new contacts; is the employee falling down on the paperwork? All these things will result in failure to reach targets or produce an acceptable return but some effort should be made to:

- define precisely what is wanted of the sales representative, ie the sales target or expected turnover, call rate, etc.

- find out (in discussion) why the employee is not achieving that target and decide whether the reasons are as a result of the employee's conduct or capability (the line is sometimes difficult to draw);

- consider if there is anything that can be done to support, help and encourage the employee, eg retraining, extra supervisory attention, etc;

- is the employee in the right job or can some alternative job be found to use his or her talents;

- reset attainable targets (in consultation with the employee) and give a reasonable review period;

- warn the employee of what will happen if he or she fails to complete the appraisal period satisfactorily. The outcome will depend on whether any alternative job could be offered and whether it is a capability problem or one of conduct; and

- provide a right of appeal to a level of management previously uninvolved if it is decided to discipline or dismiss.

Irredeemable Incompetence

In some rare circumstances the employee is so utterly incompetent that giving warnings would make no difference at all and in such cases the employer may well be justified in dispensing with the employee's services without going through formal warning procedures. Sometimes one single act illustrative of incompetence can be sufficient for immediate dismissal, ie where there are activities in which the degree of professional skill which is required is so high, and the physical consequences of the smallest departure from that high standard are so serious that one failure in accordance with those standards is enough to justify dismissal. The passenger-carrying airline pilot, the scientist operating a nuclear reactor, the scientist in charge of research into the possible effects of, for example, thalidomide, the driver of an articulated lorry carrying sulphuric acid, the driver of the Manchester to London express, are all in a situation in which one failure to maintain a proper standard of professional skill can bring about a major disaster. However, the employer must be able to show that these high standards were actively policed.

The Main Pitfalls

The major trap that an employer can fall into is not taking action quickly enough when capability problems come to light. It may be that the manager takes action too late or ineffectively, thinking that if the problems are ignored they will go away, or because he or she is reluctant to be unpleasant or assertive. General requests to all employees to work harder or to "pull up their socks" will not do as substitutes for direct individual action at the informal and later, formal stage. The "last straw" dismissal without previous formal action will almost always be unfair.

Employers should avoid being inconsistent. An employee who is warned for lack of capability but whose yearly appraisal records denote nothing but satisfaction with his or her work or who is given salary increases whilst under warning, cannot be expected to appreciate that the warning was as serious as intended. This could well make the dismissal unfair.

If the employee is given a period over which to make an improvement in performance, how long must this period be? A reasonable period should be set in relation to factors such as length of service and the nature of the job, based on how long it will take to determine whether the employee has improved. A week would be too short in most cases, whereas three to six months might be appropriate for someone with medium service, or even a year or more for someone with a lifetime of service. It is sensible to agree an appropriate period with the employee.

The employer should wait until that period elapses before taking action and the period should be extended if the employee is ill or absent from work for any substantial part of it so that a fair assessment can be made. However, the employee's progress should be monitored regularly during this review period. Notice to terminate the employment may then be given if the required improvements are not made.

Employers should not let review periods overrun without appraisal, then five months later rely upon the warning to dismiss and expect the dismissal to be fair — it won't be.

No matter how simple and junior the job, the employer has an obligation to advise and supervise employees to help them overcome any problems. Try to restore confidence; allow them to make suggestions as to changes that will help improve things or request an extra bit of help to get things into manageable proportions.

The employer should respond to these suggestions on their merits. The idea is to help employees reach the standard that is required, not to look for a speedy exit door.

Employees should always be told of the procedure for making an appeal against the decision to dismiss. This is particularly relevant where fairly junior management, who are close to the case and experiencing the inconvenience of the poor performer, have the power to dismiss. Their judgements can be harsh, inconsistent and may be based on perfunctory investigation.

Poor Procedural Handling

Failure to follow a fair and sensible procedure will in almost all cases amount to an unfair dismissal. Even if an employee's incompetence is extreme the employer should ensure that the employee is aware of the duties and standards expected. It is better to confirm this rather than assume that the employee knows what to do.

In consultation with the employee the employer may then consider possible training or even transfer to a different job (providing the employee agrees) before turning to dismissal as the final option. The employee should always be made aware that failure to improve could result in dismissal.

Ill Health Dismissals

Folklore says that employees cannot be dismissed whilst they are ill or when they bring supporting medical certificates. This is untrue. Such circumstances can constitute a fair reason for dismissal providing the employer has investigated properly and consulted the employee and the decision to dismiss is reasonable in all the circumstances.

Many different situations involving the employee's health and attendance may arise and the approach to a fair dismissal will not be the same in each. As each situation develops the procedure may need to be adjusted to suit the changes in circumstances. The employer's actions are always judged in the light of the facts of each individual case so it is dangerous to adopt a standard solution. Certain general principles, summarised in the next checklist, will however almost always apply.

Checklist: Ill Health Dismissals

- investigate thoroughly;
- consult the employee;
- seek expert advice (medical) if appropriate;
- set time limits for appraising the situation;
- explain (warn of) the outcome if there is no improvement; and
- consider whether there is any solution other than dismissal.

Doubtful Ill Health Absences

Particularly under self-certification, absences claimed as sick leave may in fact be an excuse for a day off. In doubtful cases it may be advisable to make further enquiries. The manager should interview the employee on his or her return to work, perhaps asking questions like "when did you feel unwell", "what was it like", "did you stay in bed/call the doctor/take medication", etc., in order to establish whether the absence was spurious or the genuine thing, although considerable tact will obviously be necessary. Managers should also look back on the records and see when the last bouts of illness occurred. Were they for the same reason? Did the employee go to the doctor then? (Perhaps the employee should be persuaded to go to the doctor because there is an "obvious" underlying health reason!)

Sometimes other information comes to light suggesting that the employee has not been ill at all. If the employee is confronted with this information and cannot adequately explain his or her attendance at the racecourse, shopping centre or the local do-it-yourself store then the employer will usually be justified in taking disciplinary action.

Where the employee consistently fails to notify absence properly or to provide evidence of ill health as required by the company rules, disciplinary action can be taken on this issue alone even, eventually, to the extent of dismissing the employee.

If most of the employee's absence is of the doubtful type, the manager should ensure that he or she follows a reasonable procedure before taking disciplinary action, ie:

- establish that the absence record is worse than other employees' records; ensure that the review is fair — exclude days where management has given permission for absence — and that the records are accurate;

- establish that there is no underlying medical problem by, for instance, obtaining a doctor's report (if appropriate) with the employee's permission or a report from a doctor retained by the company (see also page 38);

- if the employee has a clean bill of health he or she should be given a warning (confirmed in writing after an interview), and the matter treated as one of conduct rather than capability thereafter.

Short, Frequent Ill Health Absences

Many of the most difficult intermittent absence problems come into this category. Even though the illness or injury is genuine it does not stop the absence being a real headache for the employer.

In one case, an employee was away from work during an 18 month period for 25% of the available working time. Her ailments included dizzy spells, anxiety and nerves, bronchitis, virus infection, water on the knee, cystitis, dyspepsia and flatulence. All the absences were covered by medical certificates. She was given a "warning" about her unreliability and was told that her absence rate should be reduced to less than 7% otherwise she would be dismissed. The company doctor had advised that no useful purpose could be served by obtaining a doctor's report because the absences had no common link. The subsequent dismissal was held to be fair.

It should, though, be noted that in these circumstances the "warning" to the employee is not the same as a disciplinary warning, and may be referred to as a "caution" to distinguish it from the disciplinary procedure. However, the employee should be told how the land lies; there may be some improvement in attendance at work once the employee is aware that his or her job is on the line.

Once again, it is important to carry out a fair review of the absence record — discount days where leave was granted and bouts of hospitalisation which have eliminated the medical problem (that reason for absence should not occur again). Where there is one underlying medical problem it is important to get information from the employee's doctor (or company doctor) so that future amounts of absence can be determined or knowledge gained of future forthcoming hospital treatment that might realistically put an end to the absence problem.

If the employee refuses to give permission for the company to contact the doctor then the employer will have to come to his or her conclusions without this valuable information. The tribunal will not hold this against the employer.

Alcoholism

Traditionally, drink problems have been dealt with by employers as misconduct because of the behavioural symptoms, eg absence, poor work, etc. However, alcoholism is a question of capability rather than conduct. In dealing with it the employer should consider:

- how long has the employee been an alcoholic, and is the root cause connected with the job — for instance, has the employee been over-promoted;

- is he or she willing to undergo "drying out" treatment and can time off for this purpose be granted, either with or without pay;

- if the employee is working in a job where a considerable amount of social drinking is the norm, can he or she be transferred to another job?

However, as with any other type of capability problem, the employer does not have to put up with the problem indefinitely: if the employee will not co-operate with measures taken, or lapses back to old habits, he or she should be clearly warned of the consequences: unless there is an improvement, there will be no alternative to dismissal.

Long Term Ill Health

The employee (frequently the long service employee) who has a health or disability problem keeping him or her away from work continuously can cause a very difficult situation. Some service contracts have a clause which states that the employee can be dismissed once occupational sick entitlement has been exhausted or a period of six months has been reached. This does not simplify the issue as it would be extremely unwise to dismiss on the strength of such a clause without proper enquiry and consultation.

How long must the employee be absent before the employer may dismiss? This will depend on the nature of the job, the length of service, the circumstances of the illness, etc. There certainly is no specified legal limit. Investigation must precede any decision to dismiss. Smaller companies with fewer resources may be unable to tolerate long periods of absence. This may justify rather quicker action than would be acceptable from a larger company. Similarly, a key employee may have to be replaced quickly. The following checklist outlines four basic steps which should be followed in all cases.

Ultimately, the decision to dismiss will turn on the balance of the company's interests and those of the employee. However, alternatives to dismissal should, as always, be considered. For instance, could the employee return to take up lighter duties, to work part-time, etc? Whilst employers are under a duty to consider alternatives to dismissal, employers are not obliged to create a position for the employee where none exists.

Checklist: Long Term Ill Health

- the employer should asses what difficulties are being experienced in coping without the employee. Can the work be covered or can a temporary employee cover the job (without increasing overall costs);

- the employee should be consulted, preferably face to face, in an open discussion of the problems that are being faced.

- the employer ought to obtain current information about the true medical position. Doctors do not always tell their patients the whole truth so it is not sufficient just to ask the employee. Permission should be obtained from the employee to contact his or her doctor for a written report giving an indication as to when the employee is likely to be able to return to his or her normal job (see also page 38);

- once the doctor's report has been received, without divulging confidences, the employer should explain to the employee what effect it has had on the decision. A decision to dismiss may be made then and there or a date might be set by which the employee must be back at work.

Mental Health

Mental problems are a potentially fair reason for dismissal. Failure to disclose information about previous bouts of mental illness or the discovery of mental illness at a medical after the employee has been engaged subject to a satisfactory medical report have been found to be acceptable reasons for dismissal. Prolonged absence, gross misconduct and incompetence as a result of mental illness have also been fair reasons for dismissal.

Once again, the employer must follow a reasonable procedure. The main points to take into account are: whether the employer was aware of the problems at the recruitment stage — if so, he or she would be expected to go further in trying to accommodate the employee; has a proper investigation been carried out — for example, has the employee's psychiatrist or medical social worker been contacted with a view to discovering when he or she is likely to be fit to return to work; has the employee's behaviour led to problems with colleagues and can these be straightened out before the employee's return.

The major factor to bear in mind is that mental illness is just that — an illness — and so should be treated in the same way.

If long term absence is the problem then the employer should follow the same procedure as for long term ill health. Where employees are incapable of acting for themselves there may be a responsible person, appointed by the Court of Protection or given power of attorney, with whom the employment problems can be discussed.

Having clearly established in his or her own mind the rationale for the dismissal, the employer should investigate properly to ensure the reasonableness of the decision before the dismissal is effected. In all these situations the employer must decide whether or not continued employment is detrimental to the business, to the employee's co-workers or to the general public. If the rationale behind the decision has been sorted out and has been properly investigated, it is unlikely that a tribunal would find the dismissal unfair.

Health and Declining Capability

Another common problem is the declining capability of employees as a result of illness or injury or even premature ageing. The fear that an employee who has suffered a heart attack may have further attacks on returning to work, because of a stressful job, may cause an employer to contemplate dismissal. The employer must check that these fears do have a sound basis.

In many cases with long serving employees, another job can be found or the job may be reduced in scope but sometimes this is not possible. A fair procedure before dismissal would include:

● thorough investigation into the standard of work produced by the employee (is it substantially below par?);

- consideration of the risks to the employee's health from the workplace environment;

- seeking medical opinion in respect of the suitability of the work for the employee;

- discussing the matter fully with the employee.

If the employee's doctor feels that the employee is fit to carry out the work the employer has two options:

- to warn the employee about the standard of work under the normal disciplinary procedure and carry out that procedure to its conclusion; or

- to appoint an independent doctor to examine the employee and assess the situation in the light of the specific working environment.

Medical Reports

It is obviously important in many ill health cases to obtain medical reports on employees, but this does not mean that the employer can then avoid the responsibility for making the final decision as to whether or not the employee should be dismissed. The medical report is just one piece of evidence to take into account, albeit an important one.

For instance, if an employee's G.P. says that he or she is fit to return to work, but the working environment presents particular problems which are not known to the doctor, the company may well be right in rejecting the doctor's view. In such cases it may well be advisable to seek an independent medical view, ensuring that the independent doctor is well briefed on the work and its environment.

Where doctors refuse to given any indication of an employee's likely return date, the employee should be asked to go for a medical check-up by an independent doctor or — preferably — by the company's own doctor.

It must be appreciated that no doctor will provide confidential information about a patient: requests for information should be couched in terms of asking for the likely date of return to work; the job and any special factors should be described, and you should be prepared to pay a fee for the doctor's report. See figures 3 to 6 at the end of this chapter for model forms.

Access to Medical Reports Act 1988

Finally, it should be noted what whenever an employer seeks a medical report from an employee's doctor, the employee must agree to the report being obtained and has a right to see the report and request amendments before it is supplied. Before seeking such a report, the employer must therefore request the employee's consent and advise the employee of his or her rights to see and, if appropriate, ask the doctor to amend the report. If an employee refuses to give permission for a report to be supplied by his or her own doctor, or refuses to be examined by a company doctor, the employer will have to decide on the facts available whether to dismiss. The employee should, however, be advised of this and given an opportunity to reconsider prior to any decision being made.

Access to Health Records Act 1990

The Access to Health Records Act 1990 goes one step further giving an employer, with the employee's consent, direct access to the employee's health records. This could prove to be a more valuable way of ascertaining an employee's fitness for work than the access to medical reports. Further details of the Act are given in *Croner's Reference Book for Employers*.

Pregnancy Dismissals

A dismissal on grounds of an employee's pregnancy or any reason connected with it will be unfair. The only exceptions are where the pregnancy has made the employee incapable of doing her job or where it will be against the law to continue employing her. In these cases, dismissal will not be automatically unfair but the employer must offer any suitable available job that exists and act reasonably in all other respects (ie investigate the position to ensure that the employee really is incapable and give the employee an opportunity to present her case) to make dismissal fair.

Employers should also note that the European Court of Justice has held that under EC law, dismissal due to pregnancy amounts to direct sex discrimination.

Although an employee dismissed for pregnancy will need two years' service to bring a claim of unfair dismissal, no qualifying service is needed to bring a claim of sex discrimination.

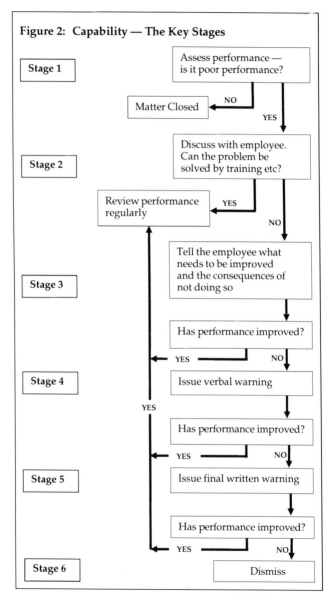

Figure 2: Capability — The Key Stages

Stage 1 — Assess performance — is it poor performance?
- NO → Matter Closed
- YES ↓

Stage 2 — Discuss with employee. Can the problem be solved by training etc?
- YES → Review performance regularly
- NO ↓

Stage 3 — Tell the employee what needs to be improved and the consequences of not doing so

Has performance improved?
- YES → (Review performance regularly)
- NO ↓

Stage 4 — Issue verbal warning

Has performance improved?
- YES → (Review performance regularly)
- NO ↓

Stage 5 — Issue final written warning

Has performance improved?
- YES → (Review performance regularly)
- NO ↓

Stage 6 — Dismiss

Figure 3: MEDICAL REPORT CONSENT FORM

I.　To: _____ (employee's name)　Date: _____

　On behalf of _____ (company name)

　I wish to obtain a medical report from your doctor/Dr _____

　for the following purposes: _____

　_____

　_____

　　　　　　　　　　Authorising signature: _____

　　　　　　　　　　Position in company: _____

II.　Employee rights under the Access to Medical Reports Act 1988

　1.　You can ask to see the medical report before the company receives it. This request for access can be made either:

　　(a)　to the company when you grant us permission to obtain it (in which case we will tell the doctor of your request, and let you know when we apply for the report);
　　　　or

　　(b)　direct to the doctor at a later date, but before the report is supplied to the company.

　2.　If you ask to see the report:

　　(a)　you must contact the doctor to arrange access within 21 days of the company applying for the report, otherwise the doctor can give the report to us without showing it to you and without your consent. (Under 1(b) above you must contact the doctor within 21 days of notifying that you wish to see the report);

　　(b)　having seen the report, you can ask the doctor (in writing) to amend anything which you think is incorrect or misleading. If the doctor does not agree, a statement of your views will be attached to the report at your request;

　　(c)　provided you have seen it, the report will not be given to us unless you give the doctor your consent.

　3.　You will not be entitled to see any part of the report which:

　　(a)　the doctor believes could seriously harm your physical or mental health, or that of others;

　　(b)　indicates the doctor's intentions in respect of you;

　　(c)　reveals information about another person, or the identity of someone who has given the doctor information about you (unless that person consents or is a health professional involved in your care).

　4.　The doctor will tell you why access to the whole or part of the report is refused. Your rights of amendment will apply only to the disclosed part of the report. The doctor will only give the report to the company with your consent.

　5.　You do not have to give the company permission to obtain a medical report. (However, the inability to obtain up-to-date medical information may affect decisions made about your employment with the company.)

　6.　You may ask to see any medical report relating to you which the doctor has provided for employment purposes in the last six months (if prepared on or after 1.1.89). Such a request should be made to your doctor.

III.　**This part is to be completed by the employee and returned to the employer.**

　To: _____　From: _____

　Company name: _____　Address: _____

　　　　　　　　　　　　　　　　　　　_____

　　　　　　　　　　　　　　　　　　　_____

　I hereby consent to the company requesting a medical report from: _____ (doctor's/consultant's name) of _____

　_____ (address)

　I have been informed of my rights under the Access to Medical Reports Act 1988. *I wish/I do not wish to see the report.

　*Delete as appropriate　　　　　　　Signed: _____

　　　　　　　　　　　　　　　　　　Date: _____

Figure 4: MEDICAL REPORT REQUEST

To. _____ (doctor's name) Date: _____

Address: _____

_____

On behalf of _____

_____(company name and address)

I am writing to request a medical report from you on _____

_____(employee's name and address),

a patient of yours.

    As we require the report for employment purposes, its provision is subject to the Access to Medical Reports Act 1988. The employee in question has been informed of his/her rights under the Act and enclosed is a form on which he/she has signified consent for this request to be made.

    We would be grateful, therefore, if you would answer the following questions for us regarding the employee's state of health, bearing in mind the nature of his/her work, which is as follows:

    As the employee has asked to see the report, the Act requires that it must not be supplied to us by you unless:

(a)   he/she has seen it, agreed to its being supplied to us and, should he/she believe it to be incorrect or misleading, has had it amended or attached a statement to it to that effect;

or

(b)   21 days have passed from the date we requested the report without the employee contacting you to arrange access to it.

    We will, of course, be prepared to pay for the report and — subject to the above mentioned time-scales — would appreciate an early reply; a stamped addressed envelope is enclosed.

    Thank you for your cooperation in this matter.

        Yours sincerely

        Name:

        Position in company:

Figure 5: NOTIFICATION OF MEDICAL REPORT REQUEST

To: _____(employee's name)

From: _____

Company name: _____

This is to advise you that, further to you granting permission, our request for a medical report from your doctor

is being made on _____(date).

As you have asked to see the report, the doctor must not supply it to us unless:

(a)   you have seen it, agreed to its being supplied to us and (should you believe it to be incorrect or misleading) have had it amended or attached a statement to it to that effect;

OR

(b)   21 days have passed from the above date without you contacting the doctor to arrange access to the report.

Signed: _____

Date: _____

Figure 6: ACCESS TO HEALTH RECORDS REQUEST FORM

I. To: _____ (employee's name) Date: _____

   On behalf of: _____ (company name)

   I wish to obtain access to your health records from your doctor or other health professional (name and address): _____

   for the following purposes: _____

   Authorising signature: _____

   Position in company: _____

II. **Employee rights under the Access to Health Records Act 1990**

   1. The Access to Health Records Act 1990 enables you as a patient to request in writing access to your health record or part of your health record from a holder of that record.

   2. The application may also be made by a person authorised by you, in writing, to make the application on your behalf.

   3. The holder of the health record will usually be your own doctor or may include the company doctor, or other health professional. Such other "health professional" may include:

      (a) a registered medical practitioner;

      (b) a registered dentist;

      (c) a registered optician;

      (d) a registered pharmaceutical chemist;

      (e) a registered nurse, midwife or health visitor;

      (f) a registered chiropodist, dietician, occupational therapist, orthoptist or physiotherapist;

      (g) a clinical psychologist

   4. Following a request for access the record holder must allow the applicant to inspect the record, or part of the record, and if required supply a copy.

   5. The period within which access must be allowed to the record is:

      (a) 21 days from the date of application where the record or part of the record was made in the 40 days preceding the application; or;

      (b) 40 days from the date of application where the record is made more than 40 days before the application;

      (c) if the holder needs further information to identify the patient or be satisfied that the applicant is entitled to apply, then the record holder has 14 days to ask the applicant for clarifying information. In this case the 21 day period begins on the date that information is provided.

   6. The holder of the record may refuse access to any part of the record which:

      (a) the health professional believes could seriously harm your physical or mental health, or that of others;

      (b) reveals information about another person, or the identity of someone who has given the doctor or health professional information about you (unless that person consents or is a health professional involved in your care).

   7. The Act does not entitle access to be given to any part of a record made before November 1, 1991 unless it is necessary to make subsequent parts intelligible.

   8. You do not have to give the company permission to obtain access to your health records. (However, the inability to obtain relevant medical information may affect decisions made about your employment with the company.)

- -

III. **This part is to be completed by the employee and returned to the employer.**

   To: _____ From: _____

   Company name: _____ Address: _____

   _____

   _____

   I hereby consent to the company requesting access to my health records from: _____ (doctor's/ health professional's name) of: _____

   _____ (address)

   I have been informed of my rights under the Access to Health Records Act 1990.

   Signed: _____

   Date: _____

4 Redundancy

Defining Redundancy

It is important to note that if a person is to be dismissed because of redundancy, the circumstances surrounding the dismissal must fit into the technical definition of redundancy specified by law. It is one of the few cases where the ''genuine belief'' of the company does not matter: if an employee is not technically redundant, then that will stand as a fair reason for dismissal. The second point on redundancy dismissals is that, even when the redundancy is genuine, the dismissal may not necessarily be fair.

The Definition of Redundancy

In legal terms, an employee is dismissed by reason of redundancy if the dismissal is wholly or mainly due to:

- the fact that the employer has ceased, or intends to cease, to carry on the business for the purposes for which the employee was employed, or has ceased or intends to cease to carry on that business in the place where the employee was so employed; or
- the fact that the requirements of that business for employees to carry out work of a particular kind or for employees to carry out work of a particular kind in the place where they were so employed, have ceased or diminished or are expected to cease or diminish.

In other words, employees may be redundant when:

- the whole business closes down;
- part of the business closes, or the business closes in a particular area and a multi-site company, for example, trades in only two towns instead of three;
- where the employer no longer needs to employ people for work of a particular kind because, for example:
  - productivity increases;
  - orders decrease; or
  - the work is put out to contract.

It comes as a surprise to many people that the last instance can count as redundancy but, looked at logically, it does fit the definition. The employer has decided to use sub-contractors instead of employees to carry out specific work and so "the requirements of the business for *employees* to carry out work of a particular kind . . . have ceased".

Reasonableness

However, even if an employer can prove that the reason for dismissal is redundancy, the second "leg" of the unfair dismissal test still applies: the tribunal must then go on to satisfy itself that dismissal was reasonable in all the circumstances.

In the past when employers needed guidance on the factors they should consider before implementing redundancies, they were able to consult the Industrial Relations Code of Practice. However, this Code has now been revoked and its redundancy provisions have not been replaced. Nevertheless as a matter of good practice (and with a view to avoiding possible unfair dismissal claims) employers should continue to have regard to the following principles:

- that, wherever possible, redundancies should only be implemented as a last resort when other measures, such as recruitment freezes, early retirement, short-time working, reduced overtime, retraining or transfer to other work, have been exhausted;

- when redundancies becomes unavoidable, the method of selection should be clearly established and fairly applied, and those affected should be properly consulted.

Of course, where a company also feels able to help redundant staff in their search for new employment or to offer advice on financial matters, such as the availability of benefits, this is likely to be very much appreciated.

As for the fairness or otherwise of redundancy dismissals, the two main points are:

Consultation

In any case of redundancy, it is most important that an employee is consulted. This really means that the employee should be informed of the proposal to effect a redundancy and be given an opportunity to comment or make representations prior to any decision to dismiss being taken. A failure to consult an employee will almost certainly make dismissal unfair. It is only the the rare case where a tribunal is satisfied that the employer reasonably believed that consultation would have served no useful purpose that the redundancy might be ruled fair.

Information to be Given to Union Representatives

- the reasons for the proposals;

- the numbers and descriptions of the employees whom it is proposed to dismiss;

- the total number of employees of each description employed by the employer at the establishment in question;

- the proposed method of selection; and

- the proposed method of carrying out the dismissals with due regard to any agreed procedure, including the period over which the dismissals are to take effect.

In addition to this general requirement for consultation, there is a specific legal duty on employers to consult representatives of any trade unions who are recognised for bargaining purposes if any members of the unions are in the group likely to be affected by the redundancies.

Time Limits

- if 100 or more employees are to be dismissed over a period of 90 days or less, then the consultation must begin at least 90 days before the first dismissal takes effect;

- if less than 100 but at least 10 employees are to be dismissed over 30 days or less, the consultation must begin at least 30 days before the date of the first dismissal;

- in any event, the consultation must begin as soon as possible.

During the consultation the employer must consider any representations made by the union representatives and reply to them, stating the reasons why the representations have been rejected, if this is the case.

Protective Awards

- a sum of up to 90 days' pay if at least 100 employees were made redundant;

- up to 30 days' pay where 10-99 employees were made redundant; and

- up to 28 days' pay in other cases.

If an employer fails to comply with these requirements, the trade union may apply to a tribunal which, unless it decides that it was not reasonably practicable for the employer to comply, will order payment of a "protective award" to each of the redundant employees.

It should be recognised that these requirements are in addition to the need to consult individual employees: the fact that the union has been consulted does not mean that the company need not consult directly with the people likely to be made redundant, before dismissal notices are given.

Alternative Work

Before making any employees redundant, employers should always consider whether there are any other jobs which can be offered to them. This does not mean that **any** vacancies should be offered, even if the employees in question do not have the right experience, qualifications, etc., nor that there is any obligation to create jobs. Employers must merely be able to show that they gave this matter proper consideration and, if any vacancies existed which were not offered, there was good reason for this.

If the new job is virtually the same in all respects (place, pay, conditions, promotion prospects, etc.) as the original one, and the employee refuses to accept it, then he or she is likely to lose the right to a redundancy payment. However, if the job varies in any way, then the employee has the right to a trial period of four weeks, during which time both the employee and the company can assess whether it is suitable. If it is not, and the employee is dismissed or resigns, the reason for leaving is, in law, redundancy. If the new job requires the employee to be retrained, then a longer trial period may be agreed, provided the agreement:

- is made between employer and employee (or his or her representative) before the employee begins the new job;
- is in writing;
- specifies the date on which the trial period will come to an end; and
- specifies the terms and conditions of employment which will apply to the employee after the end of the trial period.

Unfair Selection

There is one more way in which a redundancy dismissal

may be unfair. If it can be shown that there were other people who could have been dismissed instead of the person who was made redundant (eg if one driver is made redundant out of a team of four people all doing the same work) and:

- the reason for that person being dismissed related to trade union membership or activities; or
- the employee was selected for redundancy in contravention of a customary arrangement or agreed procedure, providing there were no special reasons for this,

the dismissal will be unfair.

Trade Union Reasons

It is automatically unfair to dismiss employees because they have:

(a) become, or proposed to become, members of an independent trade union; or

(b) taken, or proposed to take, part in the activities of an independent trade union at any appropriate time — "appropriate" meaning either inside working time in accordance with arrangements agreed with, or consent given by, the employer, or outside working time; or

(c) refused to become or remain members of a trade union.

These rules apply to all dismissals and not just those due to redundancy.

Agreed Procedure or Arrangement

Where there is an agreed procedure for selection for redundancy between the employer and employees' representatives, or a customary arrangement (ie an arrangement which is so well known by the employer and the employees that it is regarded as governing the selection), then any departure from that procedure or arrangement will make the redundancies unfair unless the employer can show that there was a good reason for his or her actions.

For example, if the agreed procedure is "last in — first out" and a long-serving employee is made redundant while an employee doing the same work is kept on, the employer will have to provide specific reasons for that decision: it will not suffice to make broad generalisations. If the long-serving employee's time-keeping or absence record, for example, is the reason, the employer should be able to produce records justifying the decision and, ideally, produce evidence of warnings given to the employee.

Time Off Work

Finally, regardless of the procedure operated before dismissal, all employees who have at least two years' continuous service and are working out their redundancy notice must be given reasonable time off, with pay, to look for new work or retraining.

The employer cannot demand proof of job interviews or the like: after all, it would be quite legitimate for the employee to use the time off to visit the local Jobcentre. If the employee believes that a request for paid time off for this purpose has been unreasonably refused, he or she can make an application to an industrial tribunal. If the claim is upheld, the tribunal may award up to 2/5ths of a week's pay to the employee.

Lay Off and Short-Time Working

In addition to conventional redundancies, employees may become entitled to leave and claim they are redundant if they are laid off or kept on short-time working (to the extent that they receive less than half a week's pay) for four or more consecutive weeks or for a series of six or more weeks (of which no more than three are continuous) within a period of 13 weeks. To become entitled to claim redundancy, employees must serve a notice on their employer, within four weeks of the end of that period, of their intention to claim a redundancy payment.

The employer may counter this notice, on receipt of the employees' claim, by telling them in writing that, within four weeks of the date their notice was served, there is a reasonable expectation of normal full-time work resuming and continuing for at least 13 weeks.

If such a counter-notice is served, but the employer subsequently withdraws it, the employee must then give a week's notice of termination (or longer notice if required by his contract) within three weeks of the date the counter-notice is withdrawn. If no counter-notice is given, the notice of termination must be given within four weeks of the date on which the employee first served notice of his intention to claim the payment.

It is important to stress that this provision does **not** mean that employers have an automatic right to lay off employees, or put them on to short-time working for up to four weeks. If this is done, and there is no agreement in the contract of employment that the employees may be laid off, then they can sue the employer in the county court for damages to recover their lost wages and/or leave and claim they have been unfairly (constructively) dismissed (see page 67).

Redundancy Payments

Employers who are made redundant and have at least two years' continuous service are entitled to be given redundancy payments. These payments are calculated on the basis of their age and their length of service (which has to be counted backwards from the date of dismissal) as follows:

- for each complete year of employment during which the employee was aged 41 or over — $1\,^1/_2$ weeks' pay;

- for each complete year when the employee was at least 22 but less than 41 years old — 1 week's pay;

- for each complete year when the employee was aged 18 or over but less than 22 — half a week's pay.

The maximum service that can be taken into account is 20 years, and there is a limit set on the amount of a week's pay which can be used in the calculation. This amount is £205 a week for redundancies which take effect on or after April 1, 1992. The limit, though, is normally increased each year. The figures from 1993 onwards will be included in *Croner's Reference Book for Employers* and *Croner's Employment Law*, or can be obtained from the Department of Employment.

The maximum amount of redundancy pay which can be obtained is therefore:

20 x 1 $\frac{1}{2}$ the maximum amount of a week's pay.

An employee is not entitled to a redundancy payment if he or she has reached the age of 65 or the company's normal retirement age where this is less than 65 (and applies equally to both men and women). If an employee is between the ages of 64 and 65 when he or she is made redundant, the redundancy payment is reduced by one-twelfth for every complete month by which his or her age exceeds 64. For example, the redundancy payment due to an employee aged 64 and seven months would be reduced by 7/12ths. In cases where the upper age limit for receiving redundancy pay is below 65, then there is no reduction during the final year.

The date of dismissal is extended for the purpose of calculating the amount of redundancy pay due when no or insufficient notice has been given of dismissal: the date of dismissal is taken as being the date that the statutory notice would have expired had it been given.

An employee may make a claim to an industrial tribunal if no redundancy payment is made.

Written Notice

Employers must give a written notice to redundant employees showing how their redundancy payments have been calculated. Failure to comply with this requirement, without reasonable excuse, may result in prosecution and a fine of up to £200. See precedent letter at the end of this chapter.

Notification Requirements

The employer must notify the Department of Employment if 10 or more employees are to be made redundant.

Notification on Form HR1

This notice, which should be on form HR1, must be given:

- at least 90 days in advance if 100 or more employees are to be made redundant over a 90-day period; or

- at least 30 days in advance if at least 10 but less than 100 employees are to be made redundant over a 30-day period.

A failure to notify the Department could result in a fine of up to £5000 unless the employer can show that it was not reasonably practicable to do so.

Example: Letter Giving Notice of Compulsory Redundancy

Dear Mrs Smith

Further to recent discussions with your manager it is with regret that we confirm the decision to terminate your employment due to redundancy. As you have been aware, the reduction in orders over the past six months has resulted in a need to reduce the workforce.

The selection of staff was based on the skills required to be retained by the Company and regrettably we are unable to find you any alternative work. You are entitled to four weeks' notice and as there is insufficient work you will not be required to work your notice.

Redundancy pay entitlement is calculated as follows and is based on your age and length of service.

Age 43 — length of service 4 complete years.

1 weeks' pay for each year of service over age 22	2 weeks
$1^1/_2$ weeks' pay for each year of service over age 41	3 weeks
	Total 5 weeks redundancy pay.
Weekly pay =	£ 205*
Total Redundancy (£205 x 5) =	£1025

*As at April 1, 1992

In addition you will receive:

Accrued holiday pay	£ . . . .
Pay in lieu of notice	£ . . . .

You will shortly receive details of your pension entitlement. If you wish to discuss any matters arising from this letter please do not hesitate to contact me.

The Directors wish to thank you for the contribution you have made to the Company during your long and valued service. We would be delighted to give any future employer a reference on request.

5 Legal Restrictions

It would not seem unreasonable to assume that, since the law says it is illegal to drive without a driving licence or for foreign nationals to work in Britain without a work permit, it would be automatically fair to dismiss someone who fails to comply. But an employer who relies on such an assumption and automatically dismisses, say, a driver who has lost his or her licence, or an immigrant worker whose work permit expires, is heading for trouble.

Absolute Proof

An employer who dismisses someone because of some legal restriction, must be able to prove absolutely that to carry on employing that person would have meant breaking the law.

Just a belief that this was the case is not enough to justify a fair dismissal. So what if the employer genuinely believed he or she was illegally employing someone, but was wrong? Well, dismissal on the grounds of a legal restriction would not be a "fair" reason but, depending on the circumstances, the dismissal could be fair on different grounds. The employer may have carried out a detailed investigation into the facts and the legal position, and might have formed a genuine but mistaken belief that continued employment would be illegal: the employer may have been incorrectly advised by a government department, for instance. In that case the dismissal is likely to be fair on the grounds of some other substantial reason (see page 71), but employers must be able to show that they were acting reasonably in relying on what they were told. If there was any question of doubt as to the legality of employment, the employer would be expected to wait until he or she could find out the true position.

General Principles

The unsuspecting employer who is considering dismissal based on the belief that someone is employed illegally should be aware of the possible pitfalls. In particular:

- it is vital to establish the true facts;

- the employee should not be dismissed automatically;

- the employer should check that his or her view of the law is correct;

- expert advice on the legal position should be sought where necessary;

- any legal restriction must affect a major part of the employee's job or an essential aspect of it;

- any alternative work which is available or other arrangements which can be made should be considered; and

- if the problem is one of complying with a legal requirement within a certain time limit, an extension of that time limit should be applied for and considered wherever possible.

It is, though, much better if the employer can prevent the problems arising in the first place and this is the issue we now turn to, before looking in detail at the main problem areas for this type of dismissal.

Prevention rather than Cure

Driving disqualification or failure to hold a valid LGV licence is probably the most common circumstance in which the problem of a legal restriction arises. Not only are employees running the risk of being picked up by the police if they continue driving while disqualified, but their employers could face prosecution too. Nor is it only ordinary driving licences which are affected. Employees will also be breaking the law if they drive vehicles without holding the appropriate LGV or PCV licences. So how do employers know whether their employees hold the necessary licences? The first check should be at the recruitment stage. Don't just take an employee's word for it, ask to see the licence and if there are any doubts about it (perhaps the validity of a licence obtained abroad is questionable) check before confirming the appointment.

Having done this, many employers think they are home and dry and expect employees who lose their licence for any reason to let them know. But what if they don't? Again, some of the liability will rest with the employer. What is needed is a procedure, set up within the company, whereby regular checks are made on the driving licences of relevant employees, so that any failure to report a lost licence will be picked up quickly. A note should also be made of any licence which is valid for a limited period. Some foreign driving licences are only valid for a few months in this country and must then be replaced by a full British licence. When the time limit expires the employer should check that the employee has taken the necessary steps to be able to continue driving legally.

Employees who do not have the necessary work permits are another illegal employment headache for employers. The rules governing the employment of foreign nationals in Britain are often complicated, but the employee who works without the necessary work permit and the relevant employer will be in contravention of the Immigration Act. Again, the best safeguard for the employer is at the recruitment stage when all candidates should be asked to confirm whether or not they need a work permit to be employed. As with driving licences, if there are any doubts about the legality of employment, check before confirming the appointment. Likewise, ensure that a procedure exists for picking up the expiry dates of work permits — preferably some time in advance.

The Health and Safety at Work Act 1974 is another piece of legislation which could justify dismissal on the grounds of a legal restriction. Under this Act, the employer's duty is to ensure the health, safety and welfare at work of his or her employees. It is not an absolute duty, but it must be fulfilled so far as is reasonably practicable to do so. It is possible, therefore, that employers could find themselves acting unlawfully if they carry on employing someone whose health, safety and welfare they cannot ensure.

Where other legal restrictions apply to specific employments, such as with the appointment of teachers, it is up to employers to check the rules and how they apply to any of their employees, and ensure that their procedures are capable of throwing up the illegality of an employee's continued employment, should it arise.

Driving Disqualification

The loss of a driving licence would seem, on the face of it, to be a fairly cut and dried situation. There is no doubt that driving whilst disqualified is against the law, but does it necessarily justify the dismissal of an employee? First of all the employer must be absolutely certain that the employee has lost his or her licence. If the employer comes to hear by word of mouth or reads in the local paper that John Smith has lost his licence, the employer must not assume that it is the same John Smith who works for the company: this must be checked with the employee.

Even if John Smith confirms that he has lost his licence, the employer must not jump to the conclusion that dismissal will be fair just because driving is part of the employee's job. Is driving a substantial part of his job? The dismissal of a warehouse employee who is only required to drive a delivery vehicle occasionally would probably be unfair, unless the small size of the company meant that it was essential for him or her to be able to drive when the need arose, whereas the dismissal of a travelling sales representative or service engineer who spends 80% to 90% of his or her time on the road would probably be justified. However, there are some circumstances in which the dismissal of an employee whose job is driving could still be unfair. Fork lift truck drivers, for example, do not have to have a driving licence so, if they are dismissed solely because they have been disqualified from driving, the dismissals would be unfair. It is important, therefore to check the true legal position.

Employers who dismiss employees for loss of licence

would also have to show that account has been taken of how long the disqualification will last. It may be for only 12 months, in which case they should look at the possibility of reorganising any driving duties to get round the problem, providing they can do so without disrupting their business. Alternative methods of transport should also be considered. Is use of public transport feasible, for instance? The employee might even be able to make arrangements for a friend or member of the family to act as chauffeur. Some even insure themselves against the loss of a driving licence (particularly where driving is essential to their work), under policies which provide such cover as chauffeur-driven transport for a limited period for anyone disqualified from driving in certain circumstances. If such a suggestion is put forward as a possible solution, some sort of trial period should be arranged to see whether it is practicable before any decision to dismiss is taken. Even where an employee is unable to get insurance because of a poor driving record the employer could be expected to check whether payment of a further premium or an increased ceiling on repairs would secure reinsurance.

A fair dismissal will also depend on whether any alternative employment has been considered or offered. Although the employer is not obliged to create another job if one doesn't already exist, failure to look at this possibility could turn an unfair dismissal hearing in the employee's favour.

Work Permits

When the employer's problem is that of an employee without the necessary work permit, a thorough investigation of all the facts is the most important consideration. The employer must be absolutely sure that to continue employing the employee would be illegal; in front of a tribunal this will have to be proved. The employer must be absolutely clear as to how and why the employee is failing to comply with the regulations and should try to get an explanation of the legal position from the Home Office and possibly also from the employee's legal representative if he or she has one. It is also important to find out whether the employee is appealing against the non-renewal of a work permit. If this is the case, the process can go on for up to a year, the old permit remains in force during that time and the employee's continued employment is, therefore, not illegal. If employers rush into dismissals in such circumstances they are likely to be acting unfairly.

Health and Safety

Where breach of the Health and Safety at Work Act, or regulations made under it, is the supposed justification for dismissal, the employer's obligations to be reasonable and look at other alternatives prior to dismissal are even greater. This is because under the Act the onus is on employers to provide a safe system of work for their employees. Any justification of dismissal on such grounds would have to centre round the fact that it was not reasonably practicable to ensure the employee's health, safety and welfare in the circumstances.

If the safety of the employee could be provided for by means of protective clothing, increased ventilation or anything else which the employer could reasonably provide, then that is what he or she would be expected to do. In such circumstances dismissal because of some legal restriction would not be justified or fair.

6 Other Substantial Reasons

In the earlier chapters of this book, the various different circumstances which can result in dismissal have been looked at under certain headings: conduct, capability, redundancy, etc. Each is considered a potentially fair reason for dismissal, provided the way it was carried out was fair and reasonable. But what if the circumstances of the dismissal do not fall neatly under one of these headings? Does it mean that such a dismissal cannot be fair in the eyes of the law? The answer lies in the fact that one final potentially fair reason for dismissal exists — ''some other substantial reason''. Just as employers are aware that it would be impossible for them to foresee all the possible circumstances in which they would consider the dismissal of an employee appropriate, so does the law recognise that it would be impossible to provide for all the potentially fair dismissal situations. Hence the deliberately imprecise phrase.

Not a Get-Out Clause

However, employers must not jump to the conclusion that this all-embracing category provides a get-out clause from the rest of the unfair dismissal provisions. Simply labelling the reason for dismissing an employee as ''some other substantial reason'' will not make that dismissal fair if it would have been unfair otherwise. The emphasis is very much on the reason for dismissal being substantial, and what employers must be able to show is that, in their particular company, dismissal was justified in the circumstances of the case. Whether the tribunal considers it justified will still depend on whether the employer acted fairly and reasonably in dismissing the employee on that particular occasion.

From this it can be seen that every case based on some other substantial reason will be different. Each one will depend on the facts and, to be substantial, the reason for dismissal must be justified specifically in the case of the employee concerned and be related to the job held by that person. General company policy on a matter may not be considered substantial if it does not justify dismissing an individual employee from the particular position he or she holds. It is obviously difficult, because of the wide scope of "some other substantial reason", to lay down general rules as to how it can and should be applied. Employers must still act reasonably, though, when justifying dismissal on these grounds and, in most cases, will have to show:

- that all the circumstances of the case have been fully investigated; and

- that other possible solutions have been considered, such as

  — transferring the employee to another part of the company,

  — retraining,

  — offering alternative work, etc.

If an employer has failed to carry out any of these steps he or she will have to satisfy a tribunal that there was a good reason for doing so and that what was done was what was reasonably practicable in the circumstances.

Dismissing Temporary Replacements

There are a few cases in which the law provides specifically that dismissal is for a substantial reason. Two of these relate to circumstances in which temporary employees are taken on as replacements for permanent workers for a particular reason.

Dismissing Temporary Replacements

- a temporary employee is taken on to replace a woman who is absent from work because she is pregnant; or

- a temporary is employed to cover for an employee who has been suspended on medical grounds under specific health and safety regulations.

In the case of a pregnant employee, it needn't be someone who has qualified for maternity rights and is away on maternity leave. Nowadays an employer is likely to have agreed to take the woman back after she has had the baby even though she doesn't have two years' service. The dismissal of the temporary replacement on her return would still be for a substantial reason.

In order to make the dismissal fair and reasonable in the circumstances the temporary replacement must be warned, when taken on, that he or she will be dismissed when the permanent employee returns to work, and this should be put in writing. The dismissal must also be reasonable which means, for instance, considering any other work available as an alternative to leaving the company altogether.

Of course in most cases, when it comes to dismissing a temporary employee in such circumstances, the person won't have enough service to qualify for unfair dismissal, in which case you might think it rather unnecessary to provide for it being a substantial reason. You have to remember, though, that this provision was introduced when only six months' service was necessary to qualify for unfair dismissal rights, and so the ruling was more relevant. You should also bear in mind that it might be necessary to justify the dismissal of someone who has been employed on, say, a couple of temporary contracts one after the other, giving a total continuous service of more than two years which would qualify the individual for unfair dismissal rights.

There are, of course, many other circumstances in which temporary employees are taken on, apart from the two cases referred to already. Since such situations are not referred to specifically in the legislation can they be dismissed fairly? Yes they can, and it may or may not be for some other substantial reason. Temporary employees must have two years' service to qualify for unfair dismissal rights but, once they have that service, the fact that they are considered temporary workers by their employer does not affect those rights. Similarly, temporary status will not prevent an employer dismissing fairly, providing he or she has acted reasonably and can justify the reason for dismissal. Generally speaking, however, you should explain to employees in writing that they are being taken on on a temporary basis, why that is so and, if possible, when the jobs are expected to come to an end.

Transfer of a Business

The third situation in which the law provides for there being a substantial reason for dismissal is where there is the transfer of a business from one owner to another. It should be noted, though, that when a business is transferred as a "going concern" and an employee is dismissed because of the transfer, or for a reason connected with it, that dismissal is automatically unfair except in specified circumstances.

This doesn't mean that if you buy up another company you have to keep all the employees, whether or not you have enough work for them to do. Nor does it mean that, if you are selling part or all of your own business to someone else, you cannot dismiss fairly employees who, say, become redundant in the meantime as a result of falling demand, etc. You can turn that automatically unfair dismissal into a potentially fair one, providing you can show that there were economic, organisational or technical reasons which made it necessary to make changes in the workforce — either that of the old owner or the new one. If you can show that this is the case then the dismissal will be for some other substantial reason in the eyes of the law.

As usual, the dismissal must still be carried out reasonably in order to be fair. In the case of a very small business — a shop, for instance — the new owners might decide that they will run the concern themselves with their own employees, so making it necessary to dismiss the employee(s) who had been working for the transferred business. As long as those employees are given fair warning of what is going to happen and why, their dismissal may be fair. The reason for it would probably be both economic and organisational — a substantial reason — and it would have been carried out in a reasonable way.

On the other hand, though, the problem might be one of transferred employees being required to change their terms and conditions of employment to fit in with the needs of the new owner. If an employee will not agree to new conditions and is dismissed and subsequently replaced, this dismissal will be automatically unfair. This is because the courts have ruled that a change to terms and conditions does not amount to an economic, etc. reason entailing changes in the workforce if the numbers and descriptions of employees remain the same.

Changing Terms in the Contract

Although a dismissal for refusal to agree to changes in terms and conditions will be *automatically* unfair if it arises from a business transfer, this will not necessarily be the case in other situations. For instance, you might want an employee to agree to move to another location or wish to increase the hours of a part time employee. If the employee is bound by a flexibility clause of some kind (in which the employer makes it clear that he or she reserves the right to change hours, duties, place of work, etc.) then any refusal by that employee to accept such a change is likely to justify dismissal on grounds of misconduct. However, if no such flexibility clause exists, the employer is not free to change the terms of an employee's contract unilaterally. If this does happen, the employee can resign and claim unfair (constructive) dismissal, or sue for breach of contract in the county court.

Alternatively, the employer might dismiss the employee for refusing to accept the new terms. Will such a dismissal be unfair? Not if the reason for making the change, and the circumstances surrounding it, can justify the dismissal on the grounds of some other substantial reason.

If an employer dismisses someone for refusing to accept a change in their terms of the contract, that dismissal will only be fair if:

● it can be shown that the change was imposed because of some economic necessity within the company; and

● before it was imposed, the employer had taken reasonable steps to try and get agreement to the proposed change.

So, the removal of an employee from his or her current place of work would have to be justified on the basis of something like a necessary cost-cutting exercise. The desire to get rid of a minor administrative complication would not be enough. The employer would need to show that it was commercially necessary, and that there was some good sound business reason behind the change. It needn't be a question of the company actually grinding to a halt if the change isn't carried out, but the employer would be expected to show that damage would be suffered without it.

It is also important for the employer to be able to back up these assertions. Anyone in this situation should check:

- exactly what the problem is;

- whether the changes under consideration would have to be permanent or temporary;

- how much must be saved and for how long;

- that documentary evidence is available to support this analysis.

Assuming a fair, substantial reason for dismissal has been established, the employer must still show that his or her unilateral action was a last resort and that all reasonable steps were taken to get agreement to the change first. So, what "reasonable steps" might be expected? One of the most important requirements is consultation; without it the chances of a fair dismissal are much slimmer.

If you don't consult, the dismissal will probably be unfair since, in practice, consultation almost always has some effect.

In the end, though, the reasonableness of the dismissal will depend on balancing the needs of the business against the employee's reasons for refusing to accept a change in the contract.

Checklist: Consultation

- talking to the employee concerned, plus any recognised trade union or other employee representative where appropriate;

- explaining clearly:
  - — the reasons for the change in the contract, the amount of saving required, and whether it is to be permanent or temporary,
  - — any alternative options available and the reasons for each,
  - — exactly how it will affect the employee;

- asking the employee for any alternative suggestions to achieve the same end result;

- allowing time for consideration of the proposals;

- listening to any objections the employee has and exploring ways of overcoming them;

- considering any alternative options put forward and checking that any rejection is for a good reason; and

- indicating clearly to the employee that the change will be imposed if agreement cannot be reached, that a refusal to accept the change will result in dismissal, and giving more time for consideration.

Reorganisation or Redundancy?

The steps you should follow when changing an individual employee's contract apply equally well when your scope of reorganisation is much wider. A substantial reason must still be established and a fair and reasonable procedure followed. There might be a slightly different emphasis on what counts as a substantial reason: the good, sound business needs must still be there, but an employer might be able to show that all the employees must agree to the change, and that the few who can't or won't agree can be dismissed on the grounds of "a substantial reason". Similarly, the only alternative to the change might be redundancy, or perhaps the impact of technology on the business is such that it cannot continue on the old basis — there have to be changes.

Faced with the dismissal of one or more employees who don't fit in with a reorganisation, you might think that they are in fact redundant. What you mustn't forget, though, is that there is a statutory definition of redundancy. If the circumstances surrounding the dismissals do not fit within that definition (see page 53) the employees will not be redundant. Naturally, some organisations can result in redundancies, for example the subcontracting of some of a company's work or the computerisation of a previously manual record system. Others, however, do not: changes in working hours from, say, a 9am–5pm start and finish to 8.30am and 4.30pm, or the replacement of part-timers with full-time staff are not redundancy situations. It should be noted, though, that a full-time employee dismissed for refusing to go part-time would be redundant, since the employer's needs for employees doing this kind of work would have diminished.

If you're representing the company in respect of an unfair dismissal claim resulting from a reorganisation you might be uncertain as to the category of the reason for dismissal. Even if you're absolutely sure that you've got a genuine redundancy situation, a tribunal might not agree that it falls strictly within the legal definition. In either case, it is quite acceptable to put the reason for dismissal on the IT3 as "redundancy or some other substantial reason". No tribunal will hold it against you, and it could well be much easier than trying to introduce the idea during the hearing.

Customer Pressure to Dismiss

Another of the reasons for dismissal which has been considered substantial in the past is that of pressure from some third party. In particular, employers can find themselves forced into a corner when an important customer or client of the company demands that action be taken against an employee. Often, the pressure is in the form of an ultimatum — either implied or explicit — "remove the employee or we'll take our business elsewhere". Generally speaking, the greater the risk of potential loss to the business, the more likely it is that a dismissal to try and prevent this will be fair.

It is a fact that, since the customer holds the ace card, he or she can require the removal of your employee (particularly from their premises) on potentially any pretext. It does not necessarily have to be reasonable. Your employees are also bound by the rules and procedures of a third party when working on their premises, and any breach of them could lead that third party to demand that action be taken, and that action may not necessarily be in line with their own disciplinary procedures. The point is that, nine times out of ten, the action demanded will only mean the removal of the employee from the third party's premises, or perhaps the replacement of that employee with someone acceptable to the third party. If the employer then decides to dismiss the employee it will be the employer's, not the third party's, responsibility.

The sort of situations in which a third party can influence a decision to dismiss can range from a beauty consultant in a department store to a service engineer for in-company photocopiers, from a contract cleaner to a sub-contracted bricklayer on a building site. If the employer is forced to dismiss an employee, he or she must first show that there was a genuine risk to the business if the dismissal didn't take place and, secondly, be able to satisfy the usual reasonableness test.

What amounts to a genuine risk will obviously vary from company to company but some possible circumstances include: the raising of objections to an employee just before an important contract comes up for renewal; the potential loss of a contract amounting to 80% – 90% of the employer's turnover; and the loss of one worth 40% of the business where only 12 people were employed.

To satisfy the reasonableness test the employer should take the following steps:

- investigate the customer's allegations or complaints as fully as possible, speak to the customer personally and check that you know exactly what the problem is. Get permission to talk to anyone else involved, eg witnesses of an alleged act of misconduct. Discuss the matter with the employee concerned and get his or her version of events, particularly if the allegation is one of misconduct or capability. The only exceptions to this rule might arise where the customer is forcing the issue and doesn't allow time for investigation, where challenging the customer might also threaten the business, or where the customer is too remote and difficult to contact (overseas, perhaps);

- make representations to the customer on behalf of the employee, particularly where you feel that the objections raised are unreasonable or unfounded. Be prepared to stand up for the employee where necessary — if you believe he or she genuinely intends and is capable of putting right whatever has been complained of, explain that to the customer;

- try to persuade the customer to change his or her mind about what is being asked of the employer (unless it is obviously justified), particularly if what is being demanded is the removal of the employee from the particular contract. Again, if the employee is being accused of something you consider trivial or unjustified try to get the customer to give the individual another chance, or assure the customer on the employee's behalf that the same thing will not happen again;

- consider any alternative work which is available. Do not automatically dismiss an employee who has to be removed from work connected with one particular customer. Look at any other work the employee might be able to do. Obviously, if there is no other work you should be trying particularly hard to prevent the unjustifiable removal of an employee from a contract. If you are unsuccessful and have no option but to dismiss, the reason should be a substantial one.

Where an employee has been accused of an act of misconduct or of being incapable, the employer who dismisses that person simply on the word of the customer will be acting unreasonably and will still have to justify the dismissal. Having investigated the allegation, if the employer finds it to be borne out in fact, he or she can, of course, dismiss the employee on the grounds of conduct or capability, as appropriate.

Employee Pressure to Dismiss

Pressure to dismiss the need not come just from customers; in some situations the strongest pressure can come from other employees. Does such pressure justify the dismissal of an employee? Is it a substantial reason? If the pressure takes the form of industrial action, the answer is quite definitely no. Employers who try to justify a dismissal on the grounds that they were forced into it, by the rest of the workforce threatening to take or actually taking industrial action if they didn't, will not be able to do so. The dismissal must be fair and reasonable despite such employee pressure — the fact of industrial action will effectively be ignored by a tribunal.

However, in other circumstances, employee pressure can be a substantial reason for dismissal. Employee pressure does not always take the form of industrial action, though. More often it is the general discontent and disharmony in the workforce which forces the employer to take action, and

---

Checklist: Employee Pressure to Dismiss

In order to behave reasonably, the manager should:

- clearly identify what the problem is;

- explain to the employee that, for whatever reason, he or she is causing disharmony within the workforce;

- warn the employee that, if no solution can be found, he or she may have to be dismissed; and

- give guidance as to how things would be improved where appropriate, eg in a case of body odour, advice on personal hygiene could be given or perhaps even a recommendation made to consult a doctor.

---

such discontent can arise in all sorts of circumstances. Personal hygiene can often cause problems: employees who smell can have a fairly devastating effect on their colleagues. Perhaps one of the most difficult problems is the objection of workers to an employee who has been convicted of a criminal offence outside work, particularly a sexual offence.

If the discontent with a particular employe reaches the stage where it is disrupting the efficient working of the rest of the company, of if the manager or supervisor has started to receive complaints from the rest of the workforce, then action should be taken.

The important point is that employers should only act on genuine discontent (unless there are other grounds for dismissal as well). Dismissing an employee in response to a criminal conviction unconnected with work, simply because you foresee possible problems with the rest of the workforce if the person is kept on, will be unfair unless there is very good reason to believe they will react against that person. Similarly, to accept the employees' assertions without question will be unreasonable. If you feel that dismissal is not appropriate, perhaps because of some consideration relating to the employee which the rest of the workforce are not aware of, you will be expected to explain the full facts to them where possible and resist their pressure to dismiss: every effort should be made to moderate their views.

Personality Conflicts

Disharmony in a company can, of course, be the result of some kind of personality conflict. Once again, dismissal because of such a conflict can be for a substantial reason, but the circumstances must be right.

One of the first problems employers face in these cases is identifying that it really is a personality conflict that they are dealing with. Sometimes a conflict of personalities is the suggested explanation for a problem at work, when really it is something else, such as capability or conduct. Alternatively, a personality clash can lie hidden behind one employee's complaint that the other doesn't do the job properly, etc. Investigation of the true facts is, therefore, all the more important and should be carried out by someone not directly involved in the conflict.

Once identified as a problem of personalities, the longer the situation is left the worse it is likely to become, so you must act quickly. Some of the things to be borne in mind when dealing with such a situation include:

- seeing the employees concerned separately and informally so that both sides of the story can be quite clearly established — seeing them both together will probably only result in a slanging match;

- trying to ascertain what the real problem is, putting forward suggestions based on what each has said;

- attempting to give each employee an insight into the other, eg "her bark is worse than her bite", or "he means well but tends to interfere";

- if possible, getting their agreement to leave each other alone and to try and get along;

- considering transfers to other departments;

- considering the relevance of training or whether there is an underlying medical problem;

- making it clear that the situation is impossible and cannot continue, that if they cannot get along together and if their work, or that of others is affected, it will result in dismissal;

- indicating who will be dismissed if the problem continues, ie the one most at fault or, if the blame is equally shared, the one whose job is less important to the company.

Other staff should be kept away from the conflict and the person dealing with the problem should avoid taking sides. Essentially, you should take all reasonable steps to try and improve the relationship or solve the problem — as usual, dismissal must be the last resort. Only if the breakdown in the relationship can be shown to be irredeemable will the reason for dismissal be a substantial

one, and a reasonable procedure of warnings, etc., will be
needed to make that dismissal fair.

Odds and Ends

Because of its fairly wooly nature "some other substantial
reason" for dismissal has covered a wide variety of
circumstances. Those described already in this chapter are
probably the ones which arise most often, but other
examples include:

- concern that confidential information could be passed
  from an employee to a relation working for a rival firm
  can constitute a substantial reason for dismissal. The
  concern must be justified and the employee in question
  must be in a position to obtain confidential information;

- genuine belief that an employee's continued
  employment will be against the law can be a
  substantial reason for dismissal, even though that
  belief turns out to be wrong;

- a sentence of imprisonment can provide a substantial
  reason for dismissal, providing it is long enough;
  likewise a period of remand in custody pending trial.

There are many one-off situations which could
potentially be justified as some other substantial reason for
dismissal, mainly because they do not fit into any of the
other definitions. Essentially, they stand a good chance of
being substantial if dismissal is within the range of
reasonable responses which any employer might make if
faced with such a situation.

7 Constructive Dismissal

In certain circumstances, employees are entitled to leave a company, with or without giving notice, and claim that they have been unfairly dismissed, even if the employer had no intention whatsoever of dismissing them. The law says that this applies in circumstances such that they are entitled to terminate their employment without notice by reason of the employer's conduct. However, this does not mean that they may leave and claim unfair (constructive) dismissal just because their employer has behaved unreasonably.

The Contractual Test

The main principles governing constructive dismissal were set out by Lord Denning in 1978. He said that employees can only treat themselves as constructively dismissed if:

> "the employer is guilty of conduct which is a significant breach going to the root of the contract of employment, or which shows that the employer no longer intends to be bound by one or more of the essential terms of the contract . . . but the conduct in either case must be sufficiently serious to entitle him (the employee) to leave at once. Moreover the employee must make up his mind soon after the conduct of which he complains. If he continues for any length of time without leaving, he will be regarded as having elected to affirm the contract and will lose his right to treat himself as discharged".

So, providing there has been a fundamental breach of contract, and the employee decides to leave very soon after the breach, he or she has been constructively dismissed (although a time lag will not matter provided the employee continues to demonstrate that he or she does not accept the change).

It sounds reasonably simple so far and, indeed, another judge has gone on record as saying that sensible people will have no difficulty in recognising conduct by an employer which, in law, brings a contract of employment to an end. He went on to give the example of persistent and unwanted amorous advances by an employer to a female member of his staff: this, he said, would clearly be such conduct.

The Main Terms of Employment

In looking to see what actions by an employer could result in constructive dismissal, the starting point is the written statement of terms and conditions of employment which should, by law, be given to employees within 13 weeks of their beginning work.

Checklist: Written Particulars of Terms of Employment

This statement should include matter such as

- the scale or rate of wages or salary or the method of calculating it;

- the intervals at which payment is made (eg weekly, monthly, etc.);

- any terms and conditions of employment relating to:
  — normal working hours,
  — holiday entitlement and pay, and
  — incapacity for work due to sickness or injury including any provisions for sick pay;

- the length of notice which the employee is obliged to give and entitled to receive to terminate his or her employment;

- the job title; and

- any disciplinary rules which apply.

A fundamental breach of any of these terms — such as reducing pay, changing working hours, varying pay intervals from weekly to quarterly, etc. — would constitute constructive dismissal if done without the employee's consent.

It should be emphasised, though, that this applies whether or not the employee has been given a written statement: such matters will still form part of a contract of employment even if there is nothing in writing. The terms will be implied into the contract.

Implied Terms

If this were the end of the matter then, as was mentioned above, sensible people wouldn't have too much difficulty in recognising conduct which could result in constructive dismissal. As ever, though, life is not that simple. In addition to any written (express) terms, there are various terms implied into contracts of employment by common law, by statute, and by custom and practice.

Common Law: Common law is "judge-made" law which predates most statute (written) law. As far as employment contracts are concerned, it operates to imply four main terms into them.

● **Pay** — there is obviously a duty on employers to pay employees for their work and this is one of the few aspects which is covered in detail before employment starts — indeed, few employees would be willing to start work unless they knew how much and how often they were to be paid. However, this duty to pay also means that if there was no work for employees to do, perhaps because of a strike in a supplier's factory or because of a shortage of work, and they were laid off without pay, the employer would be in breach of the duty to pay and the employees could leave and claim that they had been constructively dismissed, unless there was a provision in their contracts of employment allowing the employer to take that action.

● **The Duty to Provide Work** — broadly, there is no general duty to provide work — as one judge put it,

"Provided I pay my cook her wages regularly, she cannot complain if I choose to take any or all of my meals out". There are, though, some exceptions to this rule. Principally, if wages are dependent on the amount of work done or if failure to provide work has a detrimental effect on an employee's skill and competence then there is probably an implied obligation on the employer to provide work. This is why many contracts include provision for a fall-back rate to apply for employees on piecework.

- **Health and Safety** — employers are under a duty to take reasonable care for the health and safety at work of their employees. This duty is made up of three main elements: a duty to select reasonably competent employees; to provide adequate materials, and to provide a safe system of working. This common law duty has now been codified in the Health and Safety at Work Act 1974 which imposes general duties on employers with regard to the safety, health and welfare of all people using their premises.

- **Maintaining the Employment Relationship** — finally, there is a common law duty on employers to do nothing which will undermine the employment relationship. This is a vague, ill-defined duty but to illustrate its meaning, in one case, during the course of a row, a supervisor said to an employee: "Well, you can't do the bloody job anyway". The employee left and successfully claimed that he had been constructively dismissed, since the comment gratuitously destroyed the necessary mutual trust and confidence between the employer and employee.

Statute Law: There are two main terms implied into employment contracts by Acts of Parliament. The first is the "equality clause". The Equal Pay Act (as amended) provides that such a clause will be implied into women's contracts if they are:

- employed on the same or similar work as men in the same establishment;

- doing work rated as equivalent with a man's work under a job evaluation scheme; or

- doing work which is of equal value to work done by men in the same establishment.

This means that when any of the three conditions applies, the woman's contract must be no less favourable in terms of pay and benefits than the man's contract, unless there is a material difference between the woman and the man — eg merit, service, etc. (N.B. the position also applies in reverse — men may claim equal pay with women.)

The second provision concerns deductions from pay and fines imposed on workers. Such deductions are governed by the Wages Act 1986 which provides that, subject to strict exceptions, they may only be made in accordance with a written contractual term or by prior agreement with the employee.

Special rules apply to deductions from the pay of retail workers in respect of cash shortages or stock deficiencies. Any such deduction made must not exceed 10% of the employee's gross pay on the pay date when the deduction is made. However, there the cash shortage or stock deficiency is greater than this amount, the balance may be deducted on subsequent pay days, again subject to the "10%" rule. The following rules also apply:

1. The deduction must be made within 12 months of the date when the existence of the shortage/deficiency was established.

2. The employee must have been notified in writing of the total liability in respect of the deficiency or shortage before the deduction is made.

3. The employer must serve on the employee a written demand for payment on the employee's pay day.

4. The "10%" rule does not apply to deductions made from employees' "final payments" — ie the payment relating to their final period of employment or, if pay in lieu of notice has been given, that payment.

Custom and Practice: If there is no written contract, then terms will be implied by custom and practice. For instance, if employees have always been given four weeks' paid holiday a year, they will have a contractual right to this even though there is nothing in writing. If there is a contract, but it says nothing about a particular condition, then again past practice will indicate the contractual right. Where there has been no such custom and practice, a "reasonable" term will be implied by common law. The term will be that which, in all the circumstances, the employer and employee would have agreed if they had given some thought to the problem.

A breach by the employer of any of these implied terms is just as important as breaking a term which has been set out in writing. The problem for employers is in determining precisely what terms are implied — a good case for ensuring that written contracts cover all of the important conditions of employment! Examples of unfair constructive dismissals are given below.

Statutory Rights

One more point on contracts of employment has to be borne in mind: any term that aims to take away a statutory right, or to replace one with a less beneficial right, is null and void and so cannot be relied on; the statutory right will still apply.

The main rights for the purposes of this book, together with any qualifying service needed by the employee, are set out in figure 7 at the end of this chapter.

The Burden of Proof

If the employees do walk out and claim they have been constructively dismissed, it is up to them to prove to the tribunal that they were dismissed, not up to the employer to prove they were not. The employee, then, has to prove that there was a certain term in the contract of employment, and that the employer has broken that term or has otherwise shown that he or she does not intend to be bound by it. If this cannot be done, the case fails. If it can, there are then two further points which may prevent the employee from proving constructive dismissal.

The Reason for Leaving

The first point is that the employee must be able to show that he or she left the company's employ as a direct result of the employer's breach of contract, and not for some other — although connected — point. Two cases illustrate this point well. In the first case the wives of two directors of a company had a row, as a result of which the husbands became involved and the minority shareholder was told that unless he resigned and sold his share back to the company he would be dismissed. There then followed discussions between the two directors and terms were agreed on which he would leave and the company would pay him £10,000 as and when it could afford to do so.

While this might appear to be a clear case of constructive dismissal, since the company — by telling the director to resign or be sacked — was showing that it no longer regarded itself as bound by the contract of employment, the tribunal rejected his claim. His willingness to resign, it said, was influenced not so much by the threat of dismissal but by the severance terms he had negotiated with the company.

In the second case, a shop manager was told that his shop was to close — although the date was not specified — and was sent a notice to display in the shop window thanking customers for using the store and explaining that the business was to be transferred elsewhere. He wrote to his employers asking if it would make any difference to his severance pay if he left before the shop closed down. When he was told that he would get no redundancy pay if he did this, he gave four weeks' notice, saying it was imperative that he did not lose a managerial job he had just obtained elsewhere. He then made a tribunal claim for his redundancy payment.

In considering his claim, the tribunal had to decide whether he had been constructively dismissed. It decided he had not, as he had resigned in order to take up his new job, and not in response to the employer's breach of the duty of trust and confidence, and so his claim failed.

The Resignation

While the employer's behaviour must entitle the employee

to leave without notice, it does not prejudice his or her claim if the required statutory or contractual notice is, in fact, given. The important point is that what has to be said — in effect if not explicitly — is: "You have broken my contract and so I am leaving without so much as a by your leave". If an employee says: "I am giving notice and will leave in, say, one week's time" then that is alright. One woman, though, lost her claim because she had asked the company if she could be released without having to serve her full notice period. Good manners do not always pay!

Not Necessarily Unfair

However, even if employees can prove that they have been constructively dismissed, this need not be the end of the matter. All that has then been established is that they have been dismissed, not that an unfair dismissal has taken place. It is for this reason that, when faced with a constructive dismissal claim, employers should always have a second line of defence. When completing the reply to the employee's tribunal claim, there is a question which says: "Was the employee dismissed?". In answering this point in constructive dismissal cases, it is always wise to say "No, however, if the tribunal decides that there was a dismissal in law it was fair because . . .".

A good example of this occurred some years ago when the Government was operating a pay policy by refusing to award contracts to companies which gave pay increases above a certain level. One company, which depended heavily on Government contracts, gave pay increases to its employees but was then told that the increases breached the pay guidelines and no more work would be provided unless the increases were cut back. One employee refused to accept the reduction and resigned. An industrial tribunal decided that he had been constructively dismissed but it was not unfair. There was a substantial reason for the employers' action and they had behaved reasonably.

Fair Procedure

If an employer knows that employees' terms or conditions have to be changed, thus entitling them to claim

Changing Terms

Four Points to Remember

- make sure that the change is necessary, and not just a question of administrative convenience;

- explain the position to the employees, saying why the change has to be made and what the effect will be;

- if they object, listen to their reasons and try to reach a compromise if possible; and

- give as much warning of the change as possible.

constructive dismissal, there are steps that can be taken to reduce the likelihood of an unfair dismissal finding (see above).

The last point is particularly important since an employee could make a county court claim for damages from the employer in respect of the breach of contract instead of (or even as well as) leaving and claiming constructive dismissal. The only way that this can be avoided is if the employer gives proper notice to bring the original contract to an end and offers a new contract on the changed terms to take effect at the end of the notice period.

Unfair Dismissals

It can be seen from the above that — unless the employer has followed a fair procedure — the factors that can result in an unfair constructive dismissal are enormously varied. However, the main areas which have led to successful claims by employees in the past are set out below.

Express Terms

Pay: A reduction in pay is, of course, one of the most blatant examples of breach of contract. However, as is always the case in constructive dismissal claims, the breach of contract must be serious. In one case the employer decided to change the method of calculating an employee's pay, with the result that he lost about £1.50 a week. This, said the tribunal, was not sufficiently serious to justify his resignation so his constructive dismissal claim failed.

Work: The type of work that employees do may be just as important to them as the pay they receive, and so if the employer imposes a change of job on reluctant employees, they may well have a good case for claiming constructive dismissal. This point is illustrated by the case of a sales manager who resigned on three months' notice, to go and work for a competing business. His employer wanted to protect confidential information during the employee's notice period so he told him to vacate his office and transferred him on to estimating work. He left and successfully claimed that he had been unfairly constructively dismissed. The fact that he was already working out his notice did not affect his claim.

Disciplinary Procedure: The point was made earlier in this chapter that it can be very useful for employers to make the statement of terms and conditions of employment as full as possible but, unfortunately, if this is done it can occasionally rebound on the unwary employer. In one such case an employee was compulsory transferred to day duty for a two-year period as a result of disciplinary action taken under the contractual procedure. He appealed against that decision but the appeal was heard by someone who was not allowed to hear it under the procedure. This procedural defect was pointed out to the employer by the union representative and a new hearing was convened. However, this was also outside the procedure and so the employee refused to attend. He was then told that if he did not attend for work on the day shift he would be dismissed. He then left and claimed constructive dismissal.

His claim was upheld by a tribunal on the basis that the order given to him to report for day duty was a breach of contract since the disciplinary penalty was void because it was not taken in accordance with the contractual procedure. The moral is clear: anyone taking disciplinary action against employees must know the written terms of the contract inside out.

Implied Terms

Health and Safety: As was said above, an employer's failure to abide by the terms of the contract implied by common law is just as important as breach of one of the terms et out above. Two cases have illustrated this point well. In the first a woman who was required to wear safety goggles complained to the safety officer that she could not wear them over her spectacles, and stopped wearing them. She heard nothing more from the safety officer, even though he had said he would see whether the company would pay for safety goggles incorporating her prescription lens, and so she left. Her constructive dismissal claim was upheld by a tribunal because her employer's failure to investigate her complaint constituted a breach of contract.

In the second case, a woman won her unfair dismissal claim because she had had to work in a freezing cold warehouse and, on one occasion, she was left standing outside in the snow for some time waiting for the warehouse to be opened. This was the last straw, as far as she was concerned, and so she left. The tribunal decided that her employer knew about the difficulties she was working under and had made no real attempt to alleviate them.

Status: An employee's status within an organisation is an extremely important, though implied, term of the employment contract. In one case an employee was told that she had to revert from being an office manageress to clerical duties. She successfully claimed constructive dismissal. This would be the case even if there was no loss of pay or fringe benefits.

Figure 7: Statutory Rights	
The right to be given guarantee payments during a lay off for up to five days in any three-month period (except when the lay off is caused by a strike by other employees or people working for an associated employer)	1 month
The right to be paid for at least 26 weeks during statutory suspension on medical grounds	1 month
The right to take time off work, with pay, for ante-natal care and for officials of recognised trade unions — for carrying out certain trade union duties	None
The right to take time off, without pay, for trade union activities and public duties	None
The right to take maternity leave	2 years*
The right to receive statutory maternity pay	26 weeks**
The right to be given at least one week's notice for each year of service up to a maximum of 12 weeks' notice for 12 or more years' employment	1 month

*That is, two years' service by the beginning of the eleventh week before the expected week of confinement.

**That is, 26 weeks' service ending with the fifteenth week before the expected week of confinement.

8   Going to a Tribunal

Sooner or later most managers and supervisors have to appear before an industrial tribunal, whether they are there to give evidence as a witness or to present the company's case at the hearing (legal representation is not necessary in an industrial tribunal).

In this chapter we outline the procedure followed in tribunal claims from the time the ex-employee files an application.

Registering the Claim

The applicant can make a complaint of unfair dismissal within three months of the effective date of dismissal (but employees working out their notice may complain before they leave). The tribunal forms are obtained from the Department of Employment. Dismissed employees claiming unemployment benefit may be asked if they think their dismissal was unfair and will be shown the relevant forms for making an application.

When the form is completed it is sent to the Central Office of Industrial Tribunals of England and Wales (Scotland has its own office) to be registered. The Central Office will then send a photocopy of the complaint (IT1 Originating application), an accompanying letter (form IT2), booklet and a blank form (IT3 Notice of Appearance) for the respondent, (ie the employer) to complete, giving details of the reason(s) for dismissal and his or her grounds for resisting the complaint. It is important that these documents are given to the person who will represent the company's case as quickly as possible. If there will be a delay in replying (only 14 days are given) a holding letter should be sent, requesting an extension of time, to the address at the top of the form.

Failure to enter an appearance may bar the respondent

from taking any further part in the proceedings which, in almost all cases, means the case will be lost.

The Completion of the Notice of Appearance (IT3)

Obviously, it is most important to get this document into the right hands: it must be completed properly and accurately after full investigation. This investigation is vital since it is particularly unnerving to discover that witnesses have a slightly different tale to tell once they know they may be required to give evidence under oath?

The IT3 can be amended at a later stage if the tribunal chairman grants leave to do so, but it is far better to present an accurate version from the outset.

The employer's representative must give sufficient information on the IT3 to provide the reason for the dismissal and the procedure used to show that he or she acted fairly, eg details of warning letters. The practice of entering the form with the statement "detailed grounds to follow" is allowed but not encouraged.

Checklist: Completing the IT3

- check that the information on the originating application is correct, eg wages, hours, job title. If it is not, indicate this on the IT3. If it is not clear what the applicant is claiming, further information can be requested;

- be aware of what the employer must prove if the dismissal is to be adjudged fair; and

- give accurate, detailed information of the events leading to the dismissal in chronological order – WHO – WHERE – WHAT – WHEN. If there are omissions in the procedure followed explain why the steps were not taken, eg no written warnings were given because the applicant had made it clear, at the disciplinary hearing, that he or she was determined not to change.

It is sometimes suggested that the respondent should write as little as possible on the IT3, but detailed information does help the ACAS Conciliation officer (see page 101) and a well presented IT3 can often cause the withdrawal of an application. Holding back evidence on information to the day of the hearing is inadvisable. Taking the applicant by surprise with documents that require lengthy consideration will result in adjournment or postponement of the case and costs may be awarded against the party concerned.

It may be helpful if managers involved in the matter write out statements of their involvement and events (if reports have not already been made) for the employer's representative. Once again, bear in mind WHO – WHAT – WHERE – WHEN and try to place the details in a clear chronological order. The representative will also be keen to get hold of any documentary evidence that is available. (See checklist on the next page.)

If you have any of these documents ensure that they are handed to the person who is going to represent the case.

Preliminary Hearings

If the employee appears to be excluded from unfair dismissal protection on one of the grounds set out on page 6 the employer's representative should request a preliminary hearing to determine whether the tribunal can even hear the complaint at all by sending a letter with the IT3. It is also useful to indicate unacceptable dates for the hearing due to important commitments of the people involved.

In most cases a separate hearing will be called to consider these preliminary issues and the employer then only needs to bring evidence and witnesses that have a bearing on these technical matters. The tribunal will not hear evidence about the dismissal itself until the question of jurisdiction has been decided. It will advise the parties if it intends to take the preliminary points and then proceed to a full hearing on the same if appropriate.

Checklist: Useful Documents

- Job advertisement, job description, application form.

- Letter of engagement or promotion, written statement or employment contract.

- Written disciplinary rules and procedures.

- Company handbook.

- Grievance and other procedures, ie written till procedures, mandatory safety procedures, etc.

- Copies of relevant national, local and site agreements.

- Correspondence, memos, contemporaneous notes relating to the issues from which the dismissal arose, written warnings, minutes of disciplinary hearing.

- Personal (diaries, etc.) or company records, expert reports, eg medical. Appraisal reports, time sheets, expenses sheets, sales records, production figures, till rolls, etc., relating to the reason for dismissal.

- Details of wage and fringe benefits including pension details — cost of annuity equivalent to loss of pension rights, contributions of the employer/employee.

- Documents showing previous application of company rules to show consistency.

- Letter of dismissal or resignation, copies of forms sent to Department of Employment (UB85, UB95, etc.), any letters giving reasons for dismissal and references given after or before dismissal.

The Conciliation Officer

Copies of the tribunal forms will be sent to the ACAS conciliation officer. Even if respondents do not intend to settle "out of court" they should use the officer's help to get accurate information from the applicant to gain a rounded view of the issues involved. Although managers can keep their ears to the ground to find out if the applicant has got another job, the conciliation officer is usually well placed to obtain this information. In this way the potential cost of an unfair dismissal can be assessed before the hearing.

The officer's role is to promote a settlement without recourse to the tribunal. In practical terms, the respondent must be prepared to make an offer, ie pay an agreed sum, give a reference, re-engage or reinstate, etc. Sometimes applicants' cases are so bad that they are persuaded to withdraw their applications once the conciliation officer has explained the law to them.

The Effect of a Conciliated Agreement

Any discussions about settlement with the conciliation officer cannot be placed before the tribunal. Such discussions are not admissible in evidence. However, if details are blurted out by a witness, it will not go against the party: tribunals expect employers to try and buy off trouble. Indeed this is welcome since it saves the public money spent on a hearing, and the tribunal will recognise that their reasons for trying to settle may have nothing to do with the merits of the case.

If an agreement of terms to settle the matter has been completed the conciliation officer will record the details on a form COT3 and both parties are required to sign the document. Once a settlement is agreed it is binding upon both parties and the matter cannot be reopened. The agreement between the parties can be nominal or substantial: conciliation officers are under no obligation to ensure that the agreement fairly reflects the potential compensation value of the case. Only where reinstatement is agreed are they obliged to ensure that the terms appear to them to be equitable. (Incidentally, such reinstatements and re-engagements restore continuity of employment.) Where employers realise they cannot prove the fairness of the dismissal it is sensible to offer reinstatement. There is an additional tactical advantage that, if the offer is unreasonably refused, the amount of compensation awarded may be reduced by the tribunal. Any conditions agreed between the parties can be attached to the reinstatement, ie back-pay less unemployment benefit, a final warning for conduct/capability, etc.

Why Settle Cases?

Apart from the financial implications and the time involved employers must consider the effects of tribunal claims on industrial relations. Some cases will have to be fought because of important principles; for instance, union membership/activities-based dismissals might fall into this category. However, if the employer's case is poor, a conciliated settlement or reinstatement is almost always cheaper than defending a blatantly unfair dismissal. To defend it may amount to being frivolous, vexatious or otherwise unreasonable and costs could be awarded against the respondent (see below).

The conciliation officer's services are free and can be used even before a tribunal claim is made. Once a dismissal has occurred, or notice of dismissal has been given (or, in the case of constructive dismissal, the employee has resigned or given notice), then the conciliation officer can be called in to help an agreement to be reached, thus preventing the employee from going to tribunal. This is a sensible action to take because any other kind of agreement will not prevent subsequent tribunal action, although the sums paid in compensation can be offset in the calculation of any tribunal award. However, conciliation officers are empowered to act under the COT3 procedure only where there could be grounds for a complaint to go to tribunal. Thus where an agreement has been reached between an employer and an employee, without the involvement of a conciliation officer, that the employee will leave in exchange for a sum of money, the employer will not be able to have the agreement ratified.

Prehearing Assessments

Prehearing assessments were introduced in an attempt to dispose of timewasting, no-hope cases. A full tribunal convenes to assess the case based on oral evidence or written submissions from employer and employee. If the tribunal members are unanimous that the claim (or the defence) is without merit, they will express their opinion and suggest that costs are likely to be awarded if it goes to a full hearing. However, the cannot force any party to withdraw and indeed some cases have been won by the "warned-off" party!

Frequently, it is better to proceed to the full hearing rather than go to the expense of despatching the company representative to the prehearing assessment.

Current legislation provides for a new prehearing review procedure to be introduced which will allow a tribunal chairman to review the case prior to a full hearing and require a deposit of £150 from one of the parties if he or she believes that the case has no prospect of success.

Discovery and Witness Orders

If applicants feel that their employers hold relevant information concerning the case on file they can request discovery of such documentation. The tribunal can issue an order for relevant documents to be produced at the hearing or requiring facilities to view and make copies or notes of the documents to be made available. If it can be shown that the order would breach confidentiality, is burdensome or oppressive, is incriminating, concerns privileged information, or the parties agreed that it should not be disclosed, the recipient of the order can contest it. If the order stands it must be complied with or a fine may be imposed.

Tribunals have discretion to order witnesses to attend the hearing if one of the parties requests it.

Failure to comply with the order is a criminal offence, resulting in a fine on conviction, unless there is a good reason not to attend, eg knowing nothing of the matter or being in hospital.

Discovery and Witness Orders: General Rules

- voluntary attendance should be sought first;

- if witnesses agree to attend, and the requesting party is satisfied they will attend, they should not be subject to a witness order;

- if witnesses fail to reply to a request or if there is reasonable doubt that they will attend an other can be sought; and

- if a witness will not attend unless ordered to do so (eg a civil servant) then an order can be requested.

The Role of Tribunals

Firstly, tribunals hear the evidence and decide, when accounts of the situation conflict, who they believe; these then become the established facts of the case.

Secondly, they must establish the reason for the dismissal and whether or not the respondent acted reasonably.

The tribunal will look behind the stated reason(s) for dismissal — the facts of the case may support another reason. They will look at the facts that the respondent knew at the time of the dismissals, and whether, in the case of capability and conduct dismissals, the respondent had reasonable grounds for believing that the employee was incapable or had committed an act of misconduct. The respondent does not have to prove this "beyond all reasonable doubt" but does have to show that the matter has been investigated thoroughly and that the belief is based on this investigation.

When the tribunal looks at the reasonableness of the respondent's conduct it will:

- consider the fairness of the employer's actions in the light of what the hypothetical "reasonable employer" would do. It should not substitute its own opinion as to the actions the respondent should have taken;

- judge the case from the facts known to the respondent at the time of the dismissal and not on the basis of evidence that has come to light afterwards;

- apply the standards of reasonable procedures, ie the ACAS Code of Practice (see page 12);

- see if there are any inadequacies in the respondent's management approach, eg inconsistent treatment of employees, failure to train or give proper instruction, etc.

The Hearing

The first tribunal case will be a strange experience for all managers. It is a good idea to attend a hearing as a member of the public, before you have to go, just to get used to the atmosphere. On the day of the hearing arrive at the venue in good time and remember to register your name with the clerk. Representatives should make sure that they have done all the necessary photocopying because often there is no photocopier for public use. Have a pocketful of 10 pences if you expect to use the telephones. Respondents and applicants have their own respective rooms and everyone should congregate there.

The representative should go off to meet the applicant of his or her representative. The purpose of the meeting is to see if an agreed bundle of documents (evidence) can be submitted to the tribunal and also to see if there is any new evidence or a settlement is in the air. Don't be surprised if the matter is settled at the 11th hour and you can go.

Applicants do not always turn up and in that case, after strenuous efforts to contact them, the chairman may decide to hear the case in their absence or adjourn the proceedings. It is usually best to ask the chairman to take the former line or to strike out the proceeding "for want of prosecution".

Representatives should speak to the tribunal clerk before the hearing starts as he or she can give a lot of assistance with regard to procedure. The clerk will also take down all the names in the party and details of any case law that will be quoted.

When the tribunal is ready you will be called to the room where the hearing will be heard. All members of each party go to the hearing room together. Respondents sit on the left hand side of the room. Witnesses should sit behind the representative and if they wish to make any points whilst the hearing is in progress, they should pass a written note. Concentration is easily broken with too many interruptions.

Witnesses must take an oath or affirmation before giving evidence. Representatives should make sure they know the religion of their witnesses and tell the tribunal clerk beforehand. There is no need to stand whilst speaking to the tribunal but make sure that speech is slow, clear and directed towards the tribunal members.

Hearing the Evidence

The oral evidence is recorded in writing by the chairman and this tends to make the proceedings very slow. The chairman's approach to the hearing usually falls into one of two distinct patterns. Chairmen may favour an inquisitorial approach, asking most of the questions themselves and being totally in control of the proceedings or may prefer the adversarial method, allowing both parties to present their witnesses and their arguments in their own way.

Whatever style the chairman adopts, the representative has little choice but to go along with it. The normal procedure (it must be emphasised that the chairmen can decide how they tackle cases and will decide their own procedure) is to hear the evidence from one side at a time. Speaking from notes or prepared statements is not normally allowed.

The witnesses are called to take oath and give evidence one by one. The respondent's side usually starts first. Witnesses are "led" through their evidence starting with their name, address, company, position, etc. The representative should avoid leading questions but use open-ended questions such as: What happened next? What did you do? What did you say? Documents can be entered at the appropriate time with the witness being asked, for instance, whether he or she wrote the document.

Giving Evidence

Witnesses giving evidence before a tribunal will often be nervous and it may be helpful for the representative to explain to the tribunal that a witness is particularly nervous; in such a case the chairman will usually go to some lengths to put the individual at ease. It is also useful to get witnesses to talk a little about their job, how long they have been with the company and any details that help to establish their credibility, eg local JP, Councillor, many years' experience at senior management level in another company, etc.

Witnesses will usually warm up by talking about themselves before launching into the evidence concerning the dismissal. When facing experienced counsel or a solicitor, witnesses should be aware of a simple technique frequently used. A series of questions which are quite easy to answer with either "yes" or "no" is built up and then suddenly a crucial question is asked which it would be damaging to answer in such a black and white way. If pressurised, witnesses should ask the chairman to be allowed to answer the question in their own way.

Cross-Examination

Opportunity is then given to the other side to cross-examine. The chairman will help in this, and members of the tribunal will often ask questions if they need any clarification.

When the respondent's case is complete, the applicant gives evidence and calls witnesses in support of his or her version of the facts of the case. Representatives should take detailed notes verbatim if possible — especially where the facts are in contention. The company's representative must then cross-examine.

Any cross-examination of witnesses is difficult to prepare before hand but a few questions written down can give confidence and stop you "drying-up". Check through your notes of the applicant's evidence and star in red pen the evidence that is disputed. It is on these areas that you should concentrate in cross-examination if they are crucial to the case. Representatives should not try to be a Perry Mason: a low key presentation is always more effective. Chairmen are usually quick to point out any obvious weaknesses in a case, and sometimes suggest to the parties that they should adjourn and attempt a settlement. This is not improper unless there is a clear indication that the tribunal members have closed their minds to any further evidence.

The representative should put to the witness the respondent's version of the contended facts. Point out to the witness that his or her version is illogical or inconsistent, or refer to other circumstantial evidence that throws the witness' evidence into doubt.

Inexperienced representatives often receive the assistance of the chairman who is anxious to try out and assess the evidence. Effectively, the chairman will cross-examine.

If a witness is not challenged about a contended area of evidence, it is extremely likely that his or her evidence will be believed.

Don't forget that applicants can also be cross-examined on their search for a new job, their previous job history, etc., to see if they have attempted to mitigate their loss. This may help to reduce the compensation if the case is lost.

The End of the Hearing

Both sides will be given the chance to give a summarising closing statement. This is also difficult to prepare in detail because it will cover a resume of the evidence, ie outline the pieces of evidence, both oral and written, and show how they fit together to make the case. If the case has gone badly it presents an opportunity to argue that the applicant has not attempted to mitigate his or her loss or that the applicant had substantially contributed to the dismissal and any compensation should be reduced accordingly.

Representatives should make their address brief so that the tribunal can get on with making a decision. If time is short the chairman may ask you to dispense with it altogether, but you can insist on addressing the tribunal.

The Decision

Most commonly the tribunal adjourns to make its decision and will then reconvene half an hour or so later. However, the decision will not necessarily be given immediately. The tribunal will either:

- in a simple case, give a detailed decision and the amount of compensation awarded orally, with the written decision being sent on later; or

- state whether the dismissal is fair or unfair but hear further evidence before deciding compensation, either on the same day or later; or

- in a complicated case, reserve its decision with the written decision being sent on later; or

- explain that in its view the dismissal is unfair, perhaps give an indication of the likely period the compensation should cover and the degree the applicant contributed to the dismissal and then ask both sides to go out and settle privately.

If the latter course is adopted, the decision is not registered in the normal way but the case is withdrawn on the basis of an agreed settlement.

In most cases, a summary of the decision is sent to the parties but, if they request it, a detailed decision will be provided.

Reinstatement and Re-engagement

Once a finding of unfair dismissal is reached, the tribunal is obliged to consider ordering reinstatement or re-engagement. Any loss of earnings between the dismissal and the date of the return to work will be assessed and compensation awarded accordingly. If the respondent refuses to comply with an order for reinstatement or re-engagement, a basic and compensatory award will be made together with an additional award of between 13 and 26 weeks' pay. If the reason for dismissal was sex or race discrimination, the additional award will be between 26 and 52 weeks' pay. Special rules apply to dismissals on trade union grounds (see below).

Compensation

If reinstatement or re-engagement is not ordered then compensation is awarded under two headings:

1. Basic Award: this is calculated in the same way as redundancy pay, based on age and length of service. No award will be made if a redundancy payment has already been made. There are supplementary rules for young employees who would not normally qualify.

The award can be reduced if the applicant was partially to blame for the dismissal or if he or she unreasonably refused the opportunity of reinstatement or re-engagement.

2. Compensatory Award: this is based on the employee's loss of earnings as a result of the dismissal, after taking into account the attempts to lessen the loss, the degree of blame for the dismissal and an overall cut-off point of £10,000* (N.B. this maximum is normally increased on April 1 of each year). The main headings are:

(a) loss of earnings between dismissal and the date of the hearing or the start of another job;

(b) future loss of earnings arising from further unemployment or acceptance of a lower paid job (this is assessed on the basis of local conditions, etc.);

(c) loss of contractual benefits, eg pensions, company car/housing, free lunches, etc;

(d) loss of statutory protection, usually assessed as half of the statutory notice the applicant was entitled to receive.

Only rarely do tribunals compensate for hurt feelings, shock, etc. Set against these headings, pay in lieu of notice, ex-gratia payments and pay from casual employment is deducted from the amounts awarded before the tribunal applies the cut-off limit. Unemployment benefit is also deducted but it must be paid over by the employer to the State when a recoupment notice is issued.

Trade Union Dismissals

Unfair dismissals on the grounds of trade union membership or activities will result in higher awards.

The basic award is not less than £2,700 while the compensatory award (assessed as before) is augmented by a special award when the employee has asked to be reinstated or re-engaged. This is either:

- £13,400* or 104 weeks' pay whichever is the greater but subject to a maximum of £26,800* when the tribunal decides not to order reinstatement or re-engagement; or

- where the respondent has refused to comply with an order of reinstatement without justification, 156 weeks' pay or £20,100* whichever is the greater.

*It should be noted that the amounts quoted relate to dismissals which take place up to March 31, 1993. For dismissals which occur after this period, the appropriate amounts are given in *Croner's Reference Book for Employers and Croner's Employment Law*.

Compensation awarded by industrial tribunals carries interest at 15% per annum if the sum remains unpaid 42 days after the decision is sent to the parties.

Costs

If the applicant or respondent has acted frivolously, vexatiously, or in an otherwise unreasonable manner, the tribunal can award costs.

Costs will be set to reflect the amount of work the tribunal application involved; the nature of the claim; the loser's means to pay; the extent of his or her fault, and the actual costs incurred by the successful party. No costs are awarded if no costs have been incurred.

The tribunal has discretion to award costs but it is rare that the whole costs of the proceedings are given. Usually nominal costs of around £200 are awarded.

Disputing the Decision

1. Review: any request for a review can be made orally at the hearing or within 14 days of receiving the full written decision. If an appeal is also to be made to the EAT, there is a 42-day time limit for the appeal which takes no account of the impending review and must not be overlooked.

The grounds for asking for a review are as follows:

- an error by the tribunal staff resulting in the matter being wrongly decided; or

- a party did not receive notice of the proceedings; or

- the decision was made in the absence of a party entitled to be heard; or

- new evidence has become available, providing its existence could not have been foreseen, eg the applicant starts a new job sooner than the tribunal anticipated when deciding the compensation; or

- the interests of justice require a review.

2. Appeals: the EAT will only hear appeals based on an error of law. The fact that the tribunal decides that it believes the evidence of the applicant in preference to that of the supervisor is not a point of law. The only grounds for making an appeal are that the tribunal has:

- misdirected itself in law or has misunderstood or misapplied the law, eg applied the wrong statutory provision, overlooked a section of the Act or a case decided by a higher court; or

- misunderstood the facts or misapplied the facts; or

- reached a conclusion unsupported by the evidence or reached a decision which no reasonable tribunal could have reached.

It is always difficult to find an error of law, because most tribunal cases are simply decided upon the facts, ie which story the tribunal believes.

Realistically, the chance of winning at the EAT is minimal. Therefore it is essential to present the strongest and most convincing case at the tribunal hearing because there is no substantial second chance.

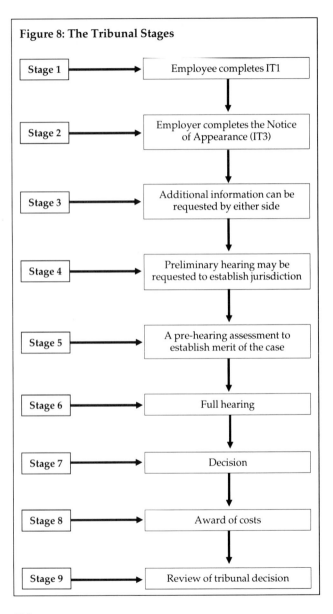

Figure 8: The Tribunal Stages

Stage 1	Employee completes IT1
Stage 2	Employer completes the Notice of Appearance (IT3)
Stage 3	Additional information can be requested by either side
Stage 4	Preliminary hearing may be requested to establish jurisdiction
Stage 5	A pre-hearing assessment to establish merit of the case
Stage 6	Full hearing
Stage 7	Decision
Stage 8	Award of costs
Stage 9	Review of tribunal decision

Further Information

Could You Use Additional Copies of this Book?

Croner's Guide to Managing Fair Dismissal is the second in a series of pocket books designed for practical use by all those with management responsibilities. If you are a subscriber to *Croner's Reference Book for Employers* this is the second of four free books on key areas of employment.

Are there other managers in your organisation who would benefit from having a copy to hand? Are you currently training your managers to handle dismissal fairly? If so, why not give them a copy to help them consolidate their knowledge and put into practice what they have learnt.

> Additional copies at a special price of £5 plus £1 p+p per copy may be ordered by telephoning our Customer Services team on 081-547 3333 quoting reference SM4.

Other books

You may not be aware of the many books we publish on subjects of interest and relevance to employers. The broad range of topics covered reflects the breadth of your responsibilities and interests.

Our books always take a practical approach and are written with the non-specialist in mind. Jargon-free language, the essential facts and a clear format ensure that these books meet your needs.

Here are some of the titles we publish:

Introduction to Employment Law
by Robert Upex
Price: £19.95
ISBN: 1 85452 063 6

Protecting your Business and Confidential Information
  by Audrey Williams
  Price: £10.95
  ISBN: 1 85524 109 9

Procedure in Industrial Tribunal Cases
  by Vivian Du-Feu
  Price: £12.95
  ISBN: 1 85525 108 0

Collective Labour Law
  by Martin Warren
  Price: £10.95
  ISBN: 1 85524 107 2

Psychometric Testing in Personnel Selection and Appraisal
  by Paul Kline
  Price: £19.95
  ISBN: 1 85524 112 9

Incentive Schemes: People and Profits
  by Ian Smith
  Price: £19.95
  ISBN: 1 85524 041 6

The Role of the Pension Fund Trustee
  by John Cunliffe
  Price: £15.95
  ISBN: 1 85524 091 2

Practical Pensions and Related Benefits
  by Ron Spill
  Price: £19.95
  ISBN: 1 85452 033 4

Debt Recovery in the County Court
  by Michael Barry
  Price: £19.95
  ISBN: 1 85524 118 8

Dictionary of Payroll Terms
  by Derek French
  Price: £14.95
  ISBN: 1 85524 162 5

For Further details contact our Customer Services team on 081-547 3333 quoting reference SM5.

Conferences and Training

Attending a seminar is one of the best ways of keeping up with rapidly changing legislation, trends and new ideas. Croner Conferences and Training have 10 years experience of running an extensive range of courses, from three-day residential to one-day seminars, all led by authoritative and experienced speakers.

Courses are regularly offered on the following subjects:

Handling Disciplinary Situations and Interviews

The Effective Secretary

Going to Tribunal

Concise Guide to Employment Law

SSP and Controlling Absence

SMP and Other Maternity Rights

The Effective Personnel Assistant

Introduction to Employment Law

Fair Dismissal — The 'Dos and Don'ts'

Employment Law — The European Dimension

Drafting Contracts of Employment

Managing People Effectively

Selection Interviewing

Managing Performance Appraisal

Fleet Management

Occupational Pensions: Current Issues and Choices

Developments in Payroll Management

For further information on any of these courses please contact Elizabeth Wolton on 081-547 3333 quoting reference SM6.

Index

Absenteeism 29
ACAS advisory handbook 12
ACAS Code of Practice 12-15
    appeals 13, 15
    disciplinary procedures 12-13
    dismissing union representatives 14
    warnings 14
Age limits for unfair dismissal rights 8
Alcoholism 41-2
Alternative work, offers of 54, 57
Appeals 15
Appearance 28

Basic award 110

Capability 33-48
    alcoholism 41-2
    declining due to ill health 44-5
    definition 33
    ill health 38-44
    main pitfalls 36-8
    mental health 43-4
    work performance 33-4
Clothes 28-9
Common law 27-8
Compensation,
    basic award 110
    compensatory award 110
Competitors, working for 24-5
Conciliated Agreement 101-2

Conciliated officer, role 102
Confidential information 84
Constructive dismissal 85-96
     burden of proof 90-2
     unfair dismissal 93-5
Consultation 76-7
Continuous service, calculation 6-8
Contractual terms, changing 75-6
Costs 111
Criminal proceedings compared with disciplinary
     employment proceedings 21, 22-3
Custom and practice 89-90
Customer pressure 78-81

Deductions from pay 87
Disciplinary procedures 12-13, 94
Discovery orders 103-4
Dismissal, definition 3
Dismissal procedures agreements 9-10
Disobeying orders 25-7
Driving disqualification 66, 68-9
Driving licences 66-7

Employees,
     consultation regarding redundancy 55
     pressure 81-2
     resignation 5
Employers' duties, common law 87-8
Employment Act 1980 10
Employment outside Great Britain, exclusions from
     unfair dismissal rights 9
Employment Protection (Consolidation) Act 1978 ..... 3, 10
Equal Pay Act 88
Exclusions from unfair dismissal rights 6-10
     age limits 8
     dismissal procedures agreements 9-10
     employment outside Great Britain 9
     fixed term contracts 8
     industrial action 9
     qualifying service 6-8
     specific employments 9

Fair procedures 23-4
Fair reasons for dismissal 10
Fishing vessels, crews of 9
Fixed term contracts 4, 8-9
Frustration of contract 4-5

Gross misconduct 18-19

Health & Safety at Work Act 1974 67
Health and safety 95

Ill health,
        absences
                doubtful 39-40
                short and frequent 40-1
        dismissals 38-9
        long term 42-3
Implied terms 87-8
Imprisonment 84
Improvement, period of 37
Incompetence 36
Industrial action 9
Industrial Relations Code of Practice 54

Lay off 59-60
Legal provisions on dismissal 3, 10-11
Legal restrictions on employment 65-70

Medical reports 45-6
Mental health 43-4
Misconduct 17-31
        company rules and procedures 19-21
        gross 18-19
        investigation 21
        principles 28
        specific examples 24-5

Notice of Appearance 98-9

Overtime, refusal to work 26

Personality conflicts 82-4
Police investigation 21
Police service 9
Pregnancy dismissals 46-7
Prehearing assessments 103
Preliminary hearings 99
Procedural irregularities 23-4
Proof,
        constructive dismissal 90-2
        incapability 34

Qualifying service 6-7

Re-engagement 109
Reasonable belief 34
Redundancy 53-63
        agreed procedure or arrangement 58-9
        alternative work, offers of 54, 57
        consultation with employees and
            trade unions 55-7
        definition 53
        lay off and short-time working 59-60
        notification requirements 61-2
        payments 60-1
        requirement of reasonableness 54
        time off work 59
        unfair selection 57-8
            trade union reasons 58
Reinstatement 109
Reorganisation 77-8
Repudiation of contract 5-6
Requirement of reasonableness 54
Right to be heard 22-3
Rights and duties 17-18

Short-time working 59-60
Status 95

Statute law 88-9
Statutory rights, contracts of employment 90

Temporary replacements, dismissing 72-4
Termination of contract, by agreement 4
Terms and conditions of employment 86-90
Theft 18, 22
Time-keeping 29
Trade union dismissals 30, 111
Trade union representatives, dismissing 14
Trade unions, consultation regarding redundancy 55
Transfer of business 74-5
Tribunal claims 97-113
        awarding of costs 111
        completion of Notice of Appearance 98-9
        conciliation 101-2
        decision 109
        discovery and witness orders 103-4
        disputing decision 112-3
        end of hearing 108
        hearing 105-6
            cross examination 107-8
            giving evidence 107
        prehearing assessments 103
        preliminary hearings 99
        registering 97-8
Tribunals, role 104-5

Unfair dismissal, exclusion *see* Exclusions from unfair
dismissal rights

Wages Act 1986 89
Warnings 14
Witness orders 103-4
Work performance 33-4
        investigation 35-6
        review 37
Work permits 67
Working in competition 24-5